# My Catholic Worship!

# DEDICATION

To our Blessed Mother. Her maternal care for us, her perfect surrender to the will of God and her powerful intercession are gifts beyond measure. May her heart shine through these pages and may her own worship of the Triune God be shared with all who read them.

# BY

## JOHN PAUL THOMAS

"John Paul Thomas" is a pen name this author picked in honor of the Apostles Saints John and Thomas and the great evangelist Saint Paul. This name also evokes the memory of the great Pope Saint John Paul II.

John is the beloved Apostle who sought out a deeply personal and intimate relationship with his Savior. Hopefully the writings in this book point us all to a deeply personal and intimate relationship with our God. May John be a model of this intimacy and love.

Thomas is also a beloved Apostle and close friend of Jesus but is well known for his lack of faith in Jesus' resurrection. Though he ultimately entered into a profound faith crying out, "my Lord and my God," he is given to us as a model of our own weakness of faith. Thomas should inspire us to always return to faith when we realize we have doubted.

As a Pharisee, Paul severely persecuted the early Christian Church. However, after going through a powerful conversion, he went on to become the great evangelist to the gentiles, founding many new communities of believers and writing many letters contained in Sacred Scripture. His letters are deeply personal and reveal a shepherd's heart. He is a model for all as we seek to embrace our calling to spread the Gospel.

# *My Catholic Life! Series*

## An introduction to this three volume series

The *My Catholic Life! Series* is a three volume series written as a complete summary of our glorious Catholic faith! The goal of these books is to answer the difficult and deep questions of life in a clear and understandable way. We need to know who we are and what life is all about. We need to know who God is and what He has spoken to us through the ages.

Volume One, *My Catholic Faith!* is a summary of the Apostles' and Nicene Creeds. This volume looks at everything from the creation of the world to God's eternal plan of salvation. Other topics include: The afterlife, the Trinity, saints, our Blessed Mother, faith, and the Church. It is a summary of the teaching of the *Catechism of the Catholic Church* #1-1065.

Volume Two, *My Catholic Worship!* is a summary of the life of grace found in prayer and the Sacraments. So often the Sacraments can be seen as dry and empty rituals. But they are, in reality, the greatest treasures we have! They are God's true presence among us! This book is a summary of the *Catechism of the Catholic Church* #1066-1690 and #2558-2865.

Volume Three, *My Catholic Morals!* is a summary of Catholic moral teaching. It reveals the moral principles of our faith as well as a summary of all our Church's moral teachings. It is a summary of the *Catechism of the Catholic Church* #1691-2557.

# Table of Contents

# Introduction

We are called to love the Lord our God with our whole heart, mind, soul and strength (see Matthew 22:37). This is not an option if we want to be a Christian! It's a command of love from God and is an invitation to share in His divine life. We should hear those words and soak them up desiring to fulfill them in our daily life.

How do we do this? How do we love God with everything we are? To say with all your "heart, mind, soul and strength" means everything! It means all that we are. Our whole being. So loving God in the way we are called to requires a very radical commitment on our part. It requires that we are "all in" so to speak. So, again, how do we do this?

The key is worship! To worship God is to love God in the way we are called to love. To worship God means that He is indeed the God of our life and nothing else gets in the way. It means we allow our heart, soul and mind to become immersed in God and filled with His presence. This is worship. And it's our calling in life.

To worship God requires two basic things. It's very simple. First, it requires God acting on us. This means He speaks, He calls to us, and He invites us into His life of grace. So worship is first and foremost an act of God in our lives. Second, worship is us responding to that incredible invitation. It's us saying yes to God. Yes to His invitation and yes to His will. This is done especially in surrender. Surrender to that glorious invitation from a God who loves us more than we can imagine!

Worship is prayer. It's true prayer. But it's not only a prayer we offer at church or at a specific prayer time. Rather, we are called to worship God 24/7 in all that we do and all that we are. We cannot set specific times of worship and times when we do not worship. It's a calling to constantly be in God's presence surrendering all to Him.

With that said, it's also important to point out that each of us needs time, each and every day, and especially on Sunday, set aside ONLY for direct worship of God. Yes, we must strive to continually live in His presence responding to His will each and every moment, but to do that well we need time when that's all we do. We need time to silence all other activities of life and give all our attention to the direct love and worship of our God. If we do that well, we will more easily be able to bring God's presence into our daily lives.

This book is about Worship of the Triune God! There is nothing more important in life than what is presented here in these pages. Not because of this book itself, but because of the truths this book shares.

There are two main sections of this book. The first section is about prayer as it is lived in the Sacraments of our Church. The Sacraments can seem, at times, to be dry, dull and repetitive. They can, at times, feel like empty rituals that we are "obliged" to do out of obedience. But when understood and entered into correctly, the Sacraments become the greatest source of our intimacy with our God. They become personal. They become *My Catholic Worship!*

The second section of this book deals with all other forms of prayer. It highlights various methods as well as the meaning of prayer. So jump into this book with an open heart and know that God wants to draw you more closely to Himself in all forms of worship. He wants you to know and love Him with your whole heart, mind, soul and strength. And the way to do just that is prayer!

> For me, prayer is a surge of the heart; it is a simple look turned toward heaven, it is a cry of recognition and of love, embracing both trial and joy (St. Thérèse of Lisieux, Manuscrits autobiographiques, C 25r). (*CCC* #2558)

# 1

# THE GREATEST ACT ON EARTH

If we were to make a list of everything in the world that is truly priceless, what would that list look like? A few things that come to my mind would be the Grand Canyon, Niagara Falls, and the Teton Mountains. These are spectacular and awe-inspiring gifts from Nature that are unmatched in beauty and majesty by any human endeavor. If we were to expand the list to some of the most amazing accomplishments of humanity, the list may include the Opening Ceremonies of the Olympic Games, a Super Bowl halftime show, or a top notch Hollywood production. The time, money and talent put into these events are astonishing to think about. Perhaps you have other ideas that you can add to the "priceless" list. What would that list look like? Would it include something as familiar as the Catholic Liturgy?

The Liturgy, without a doubt, is THE most amazing event that has ever taken place in this world. Don't you agree? Or is this a doubtful comment to make? But if we understand the Liturgy, we'd realize that it will continue to be the greatest event until the end of time. It is more than any mere human endeavor or gift of nature. It is a divine reality that we are infinitely privileged to participate in. Unfortunately, we often simply do not realize this truth.

Now before you dismiss this idea as some overly pious thought, or simply as a way to get you to read more of this book, I encourage you to commit yourself to an in-depth reflection on this amazing event of the Liturgy. Try to take a look at it with new eyes. Try to be open to new possibilities and a new understanding. If you do, you may just find that you will make the greatest discovery you could ever make!

## The Great *Mysterium Fidei*

So what is the Liturgy? Is it just some dry set of actions we have to watch and participate in each Sunday out of an obligation? Is it simply our "duty" toward God? Or is it more? The truth is that it is the greatest mystery on Earth. It is the *Mysterium Fidei*, the great "Mystery of Faith." As a "mystery," the Liturgy is something that we must strive to understand, while also realizing it is something we can never comprehend. Let me say it this way: As a "mystery," the Liturgy has unlimited potential to draw us in and change our lives. But, as with any mystery, it is unimpressive if we look at it in a confused and puzzled way. If we just see the externals we may be impressed to a small extent. For example, if the music is extraordinary, the art in the Church is glorious or the homily is enthralling, we may walk away impressed. But if we settle for these aspects of the Liturgy alone, and make them our barometer by which we measure its value, then we have misunderstood the Liturgy and have not begun to penetrate the great mystery that it is.

Let me offer an analogy. We can say that each person we encounter is a mystery. Some may seem more mysterious than others but each of us is a mystery. This must be properly understood. By saying that each person is a "mystery" we mean that it's impossible to ever say, in a definitive way, "I know everything about that person!" No, that's not possible. It is possible to understand another person but only to a limited degree. For example, a husband and wife who have had a wonderful marriage for 50+ years will be able to say they know each other exceptionally well. But even in this case it's never possible to say that they *fully* know each other. Why? Because the depth and complexity of who we are is something known only to God. We cannot even understand ourselves completely!

With this understanding, we must also realize that if we cannot fully comprehend and "figure out" another person, then we will never be able to fully figure out God and His workings. And among the things we will never fully figure out is His action we call the Sacred Liturgy! But we must try to at least enter in as deeply as we can to an understanding of this great gift. We must try to understand God as He is and as He makes Himself manifest to us through these sacred actions.

## Liturgy 101

Let's do some basic catechesis to get the big picture of the Liturgy. Try to be extra attentive to these basic descriptions of the Liturgy so that you have a basis for the rest of this book. No, this catechesis is not boring, but it does require some concentration, so ponder this catechesis extra hard.

The Liturgy is an action of both Christ and His Church. In the previous book we reflected upon how the Scriptures were 100% the work of God as well as 100% the work of the human author. We also acknowledged that Jesus was 100% God and 100% human. The Liturgy is the same way. The Liturgy is 100% the working of God and 100% a work of the Church. It's an action that is joined as if married together and united as one. It's a joint effort of God and His Church!

**An Action of God:** *As an action of God*, the Liturgy is especially an action of Christ, the High Priest offering His life for the salvation of the world. This is a key concept to understand! Jesus offered His life on the Cross for the salvation of the world once and for all almost 2000 years ago. That one saving act was His priestly act of atoning for our sins by offering Himself both as the High Priest AND as the Victim. He is the one offering the sacrifice and He IS the sacrifice He offers.

**Role of Jesus the Son:** The key to understanding the Liturgy is to realize that the action Jesus did, so long ago, was not just a onetime historical *event* that we now look back at and are grateful for. Yes, it was a "onetime" historical event, but it is also a perpetual event. That sacrifice of Jesus long ago is an action that transcends all time and permeates all things. This is a deep concept but it must be understood if we are to understand the Liturgy. You see, with God there is no time. This means that He is able to take this one event that took place *within time* and apply it to people *of every time*. And this is accomplished first and foremost within the Sacred Liturgy.

It's as if the Liturgy allows us to enter into a time machine every time we participate. And that time machine transports us to the moments of Christ's Incarnation, His preaching, His death on the Cross and His resurrection all at once! So the Liturgy is, strictly speaking, a "timeless" reality. It transcends all of time bringing Jesus' saving actions to meet us here and now. The Liturgy, as an action of Christ, is the perpetual "making present" to us His work of salvation: His incarnation, death and resurrection. The Liturgy becomes the vehicle through which all that Jesus accomplished is now transmitted to us. It's the channel of that grace in every day and age. It's the instrument by which we receive that action of Jesus. And, in fact, it IS that one action of Jesus! This Liturgy is God's living action of salvation. Again, this is a great mystery, but we must do all we can to comprehend it as fully as we can. Even if it stretches our brain a bit!

We also want to acknowledge the role of the Father and the Holy Spirit in the Liturgy. And to understand this, all we have to do is understand the role of the Father and the Holy Spirit in the original act of salvation that Jesus accomplished.

**Role of the Father in the Perpetual Liturgy:** Jesus was Incarnate in accord with the will of the Father. He lived in perfect union with, and in obedience to, the Father's will. It was the Father's will that Jesus live His life, embrace the Cross and offer His life for the salvation of the world. It is this perfect cooperation with the will of the Father that gives the greatest glory to God the Father. Thus, *Jesus' act on the Cross was an act that gave perfect honor and glory to the Father.* And so it is with the Liturgy. The Liturgy, as a continual re-presentation of the one act of Christ on the Cross, is, therefore, an act that gives perfect honor to the Father! Since the action of the Cross and the Liturgy are one act, all that the Cross accomplishes is also applied to the Liturgy. Therefore, the Liturgy is an act of perfect obedience to the will of the Father thus giving Him perfect glory and honor. And when we participate in the Liturgy, we share in this honoring and glorifying of the Father.

Are you still following? This is a very deep and mysterious concept to understand. But it's all true and it is worth reading and re-reading so that we understand. Well, understand at least as much as is possible! It still remains a mystery which means that, even though we can understand, we will never fully comprehend.

**Role of the Holy Spirit in the Perpetual Liturgy:** The Holy Spirit is also an actor in the Liturgy. The Holy Spirit's role in the Liturgy is exactly the same as it was for the life, death and resurrection of

Christ. Again, this onetime historical act of Christ and the perpetual Liturgy are one and the same act. For that reason, the role of the Holy Spirit also plays one and the same role in each.

We will remember that it was by *the Holy Spirit* that the eternal Son became man in the womb of the Virgin Mary (Luke 1:31). It was the Holy Spirit who descended upon Jesus at His baptism. The Holy Spirit was present with Jesus through His betrayal, suffering and death. And at that last moment on the Cross Jesus "gave up His Spirit." The Holy Spirit was also promised by Jesus after His resurrection and descended upon the Church at Pentecost. Thus, the Holy Spirit was integrally involved in all aspects of the onetime act of salvation and is, therefore, integrally involved in all aspects of the perpetual Liturgy. Christ gave the Holy Spirit to the Church and the Holy Spirit now continues to keep this saving sacrifice of Christ alive in every day and age in the Liturgy.

**An Action of the Church:** In addition to the Liturgy being an action of God, *it is also an action of the Church.* It is both for the Church and by the Church. It is *by* the Church in the sense that the Church Herself is the visible presence of Christ in our world. What does this mean? The Church itself can be called a "Sacrament." The Church is a sacrament in the sense that Christ is fully present through the Church and we, the members of the Body of Christ, are wedded to Him. Thus, His actions in our world come through His body according to their various roles and ministries. His Incarnation and saving act continues to be made present through the ministry of the Church. Therefore, when the Liturgy is celebrated it is an action of Christ done *by* the Church, through the action of the Church's ministers in which the laity participates.

The Liturgy is also *for* the Church in the sense that it is the food of His Word and grace that is communicated to all the members. The Church (specifically all of us who are members of the Church) is given Christ Himself in the Liturgy and is, therefore, made holy through participation in the Liturgy. So, that which Christ accomplishes and presents through the Church is also *for* those members of that very Church. The grace given is for us and by us according to our various roles. Hopefully this makes sense, at least a little. And hopefully it is truly an inspiring and exciting reality to consider.

To sum it up, the Liturgy is both an action of Christ and His Church, acting as one, to communicate all that Jesus did for us by His life, death and resurrection. This is the gift of salvation. And this gift of salvation is an ongoing gift which we receive to a greater and greater degree, in time and space, each time we participate in the Liturgy. For it is there, in the Liturgy, that we meet our God and are transformed by Him. The Liturgy is the most excellent means by which this happens and is, therefore, the greatest form of prayer there is.

## Is the Liturgy Boring?

Let's be honest. Some may feel that the Liturgies they have participated in are boring. Be it the Mass itself, any other sacrament, Benediction of the Blessed Sacrament, or any other form of liturgical worship, it's possible for us to be bored. Sure, the priest may lack devotion and even faith. His homily may not connect with us. But if we truly understood the Liturgy we would not let any of that bother us! If we understood the divine reality taking place, we would truly meet Christ in every liturgical action and grow in daily grace. This is harder when the Liturgy is celebrated poorly for sure. But it's never impossible and must be our constant goal.

The priest, on his part, has a sacred duty to enter into the Liturgy and offer it well. His faith-filled celebration will also encourage others participating to offer their participation well. But strictly speaking, a "poor" celebration of the Liturgy by a priest (meaning a poor homily or lack of sincere devotion), is, in some ways, actually an invitation to us to enter in more deeply. Yes, a poor celebration on the part of the priest can actually be cause for those participating to celebrate with even greater faith and devotion. Why is this the case? Because it requires the participant to see beyond the more superficial aspects of the Liturgy, and engage this worship on a deeper level. It means entering in with a more purified faith believing not so much because we are drawn in by the celebrant, or by the music, or by the environment, but because we are drawn by faith into what is happening. We believe *despite* any lacking on the part of those around us. This is hard to do, but it's right and good that we strive for this level of faith every time we participate in various liturgical celebrations.

To celebrate the Liturgy, specifically the Sacraments, we need to understand that they accomplish their purpose whether we are paying attention or not. There is an old Latin phrase used to communicate this idea. The phrase is that the Sacraments work: *ex opere operato* (by the very fact of the actions being performed). In other words, when a sacrament is celebrated, the mystery spoken of above takes place whether we are engaged in it or not. The mystery is made present even if the priest is not that engaged or engaging! So, again, it's not a matter of how entertaining the priest and the choir are, it's a matter of knowing, with a deep and certain faith, that the Sacraments do what the Church says they do. If we believe this, it will make our participation in every sacrament more effective in our lives.

Another area to look at is the effect that the Liturgy has on our faith. There is another old Latin saying in the Church which points to the relationship between our faith and our worship. The phrase is: *lex orandi, lex credenda*. This literally means, "The law of prayer is the law of faith." This happens on the universal level as well as a personal level. We are taught objective truths about the faith through the Liturgy and grow personally in faith by our participation in the Liturgy. For example, the Mass is passed down as a very clear and set liturgical rite. As a result, matters of faith are also communicated to us through it. We come to discover the meaning of the Mass and grow in faith as a result. The way we worship in the Mass teaches us our faith, forms us in faith and enables us to live that faith. For example, when the priest genuflects, after he consecrates the bread and wine into the Body and Blood of Christ, we are taught a lesson of faith through this action. We are taught that Christ is truly present. That He deserves our adoration in that moment. So we learn our faith from the actions of the Liturgy. The same is true with every other liturgical action. The Liturgy teaches us our faith, AND it contains our faith. To understand the Liturgy, therefore, is to understand our faith. Understanding what we do in the Liturgy enables us to know what we, as a Church, believe.

## Who Celebrates the Liturgy?

The Liturgy is a celebration of all the members of the Church. It is therefore a celebration of Jesus, the choir, presider, lector, servers, and all the faithful attending. It is an action of the whole Church from head to heart to toe! The entire Body of Christ is celebrating.

One of the most common phrases from Vatican II, regarding the Liturgy, is that there must be a "conscious, active, and fruitful participation" of everyone (See *Catechism* #1071). This means that the Liturgy is not just something people attend, it's something they do. It's an action of the whole Church, with each person exercising his or her unique role. And, above all, the role common to every person is an authentic *interior* participation (not just exterior) in the worship.

After Vatican II, the phrase "conscious, active, and fruitful participation" was commonly misunderstood to mean that everyone had to have an official or formal part in the Liturgy. And if you did have an official part, you were somehow fulfilling your baptismal calling more completely. The problem with this is that, if you didn't have an official part, were you participating less? Certainly not. Participation is first and foremost interior or active engagement in the worship of God taking place in the Liturgy. Certainly there are some roles that need to be filled (lectors or choir for example). And these roles are integral to the Liturgy. But don't let yourself be misled into thinking that fulfilling one of these roles makes you a more "conscious, active and fruitful" participant. Active and fruitful participation is achieved when your heart is engaged and you participate with faith. This is the primary goal of our worship.

Among the roles within the Liturgy there is certainly one that is essential. This is the role of the ordained minister. The ordained minister, especially in the celebration of the Eucharist, acts *in Persona Christi*, in the Person of Christ. This doesn't mean that the priest, for example, has attained some special height of holiness. Hopefully that's the case also. What it means is that, in the person of the priest, Christ Himself is present offering the sacrament. This happens by virtue of his ordination. And this is essential since the Liturgy is an action of both Christ and His Church. So Christ is there, in the person of the priest, and He is also there, in the grace that is given.

## How the Liturgy is Celebrated

Prayer, in and of itself, is something internal. It's an encounter with the living God in our soul. It requires no special exterior help since God can communicate to us any way He chooses. But the Liturgy, being both an interior act of each participating member and a public act of the Church, requires a certain external aspect. This is especially seen in the various signs and symbols we use in our celebrations. The signs and symbols used within the liturgical celebrations are many. More will be said on them in the chapters on each particular sacrament. But as a brief illustration, here are a few of the ways we use signs and symbols in the Liturgy:

- Certain colors are used for each liturgical season. Each color has a specific symbolic meaning:
  - White is used in the seasons of Christmas and Easter as well as other special celebrations within the Church: Trinity Sunday, Corpus Christi, feasts of our Lord, feasts of our Blessed Mother, feasts of the saints (unless they are martyrs), feasts of the angels, weddings and funerals. White symbolizes purity, holiness, rejoicing, triumph, glory and new life.
  - Red is used for feasts of the Holy Spirit, feasts of the precious blood, the passion and feasts of martyrs. Red symbolizes blood and fire.
  - Violet is used in Advent and Lent and is a symbol of penance, sorrow and mortification.
  - Green is used in Ordinary Time and is a symbol of ongoing hope and conversion in our daily life.
  - Black can be used for funerals and other Masses for the dead and symbolizes mourning.
  - Rose is used the third Sunday of Advent and the fourth Sunday of Lent and is a form of violet with the added emphasis of joy. Therefore, it symbolizes the end of the penitential season is in sight.
  - Gold can be used whenever white is used, especially for very special feasts. It symbolizes great joy.
- We use incense which is an offering of reverence as well as a sign of our prayers rising to Heaven.
- The ambo (pulpit) is fixed and prominent to give dignity to the Word of God.

- The altar is also fixed and central to show the centrality of the Eucharist.
- Sacred art points us to the Heavenly realities.
- Sacred music is the highest form of art since it uses the human voice.
- Bread and wine are signs of what they <u>actually</u> become, namely, the Body and Blood of Christ. The use of bread symbolizes that Christ's Body provides our basic sustenance. The use of wine for His Blood symbolizes that the Eucharist draws us to a life of superabundance.
- Oil is a sign of what it actually does – anoints with the Holy Spirit.
- Genuflection – When we come into church we genuflect (go down on one knee) as a sign of reverence toward the Blessed Sacrament present in the tabernacle.
- The sign of the Cross is made and symbolizes the sacrifice of Christ. It also symbolizes the fact that we are signed with that Cross and covered in His Blood and is made with a Trinitarian response (In the name of the Father...) uniting the Crucifixion with the Trinity.

These are only a few among the many signs and symbols we use in the various liturgies of our Church. Signs and symbols are used because we live in a material world. And by the fact that God entered this material world, creation is able to reflect and share in His redeeming activity. We are physical people with five senses. Those five senses enable the use of signs and symbols for divine purposes. And this is what is accomplished in the Liturgy!

Signs and symbols were used by God throughout the history of the world. We see in the Scriptures many examples:

- The dove that returned to Noah;
- The Burning Bush encountered by Moses;
- The pillar of fire and clouds leading Israel to freedom;
- The anointing of the Old Testament Kings;
- The act of circumcision;
- The Temple and the Old Testament liturgical rites;

- The water used by John the Baptist;
- The dove that descended on Jesus;
- The light radiating from Jesus at the Transfiguration, etc.

So it is with the Liturgy. There are countless ways we use the material world of signs and symbols, as well as words and actions, to cooperate with the divine action of God. It is through these signs, symbols, words and actions that God is made present to us and we receive His gift of grace and salvation.

With the above brief reflection on the many signs and symbols used in liturgical worship, we must make one more very important point. The signs and symbols used in the Liturgy, especially the Sacraments, actually bring about what they signify. In other words, the liturgy is not just symbolic. Rather, the reality of worship takes place and God is made present through these signs and symbols. The oil actually brings the Holy Spirit, the water actually cleanses sins, the bread and wine actually become Christ Jesus, etc. This reveals the beauty and power of the Liturgy!

**When Do We Celebrate?**

It would be easy to miss the great meaning of the liturgical year and, what we may call, the "liturgical week." By "liturgical year" we point to the fact that our Church commemorates every aspect of Jesus' work of salvation over the course of an entire year. We begin with Advent, focusing on the Incarnation and birth of Christ at Christmas. We celebrate the suffering and death of Christ in Lent. And we rejoice in His Resurrection at Easter. Ordinary time is an opportunity to enter into the daily life of Christ, His teachings and His ministry.

Though this is not an official phrase used in the Church, we could also speak of the "liturgical week" insofar as we set aside Sunday as the Lord's Day and as a holy day of obligation. Friday is traditionally used as a day of fast and a day to ponder the mystery of Christ's death. And Saturday is often dedicated to the honor of our Blessed Mother.

In addition to these set celebrations there are many other solemnities, feasts, memorials and days in which we honor specific saints or articles of our faith. It's all there, each and every year, within the glorious life of our Church's worship!

**Where Do We Celebrate?**

The place of worship could be any place on Earth insofar as all of creation is a gift from God and a fitting place of worship. But a church is a special place set aside solely for the purpose of divine worship. And within the church building there are various dedicated structures that are used solely for the purpose of the Liturgy. Here are a few examples:

- The altar is to be used only for the Mass, and nothing else;
- The ambo is to be used only for the proclamation of the Word of God and prayers, but nothing else. It is to be solid, prominent, immovable and in an elevated position. The actual word signifies a mountain or elevation. It's appropriate to see it as an elevated "mountain" where the Word of God is preached;
- The sanctuary is set aside as the "holy of holies" within the church building;
- The presider's chair is used only by the presider and enables the priest to sit in this prominent position to image Christ presiding as head of the Church.
- The tabernacle is to be in the church's most worthy and prominent place to signify what it contains – Jesus Himself!

And there are other parts of a church set aside for a specific liturgical function. Having a special place to celebrate the Liturgy adds dignity and clarity to the sacredness of the celebration. We do not simply use an ordinary space since it is no ordinary action. Furthermore, the entire church is set up to signify the Body of Christ, both body and head. The gathering people are His body and the priest acts in the person of Christ the Head.

Lastly, the church itself is a sign of the Heavenly reality. When we enter the church this signifies our passage from the world to God and

His sanctuary in Heaven. We cross the threshold and leave sin behind. So the church building itself is a sign of our journey and entrance into the glories of Heaven!

## Diversity vs. Unity

The last general principle of the Liturgy we will focus on, before looking specifically at the Sacraments, is the fact that there are many liturgical rites that have developed over the centuries. The older generation will remember that the Mass used to be celebrated according to the Tridentine Rite. This is casually referred to by some as "the Mass celebrated in Latin with the priest's back to the people." This is the way the Mass was celebrated for centuries.

Additionally, there are numerous other liturgical rites within the Church which we call the "Eastern Catholic Rites." The rite that most Catholics celebrate in the United States and other countries is the Latin Rite. But in addition to this rite there are the following within our Church: Byzantine, Alexandrian or Coptic, Syriac, Armenian, Maronite and Chaldean rites. Some religious orders even have their own unique rites. Each of these rites evolved over the centuries in certain places and cultures. All of them are good and beautiful. Each of them celebrates the same Mass and proclaims the same faith. But they are each different in their expression.

Each one of these rites may use a specific language, follow special liturgical norms, use unique symbols and words, etc. Though the expression is diverse, the faith and worship is the same. Therefore the unity is sustained. And, in fact, the diversity experienced by the Church through the various liturgical rites actually has the effect of uniting us more closely. Why? Because our unity is not so much the result of uniformity but results from our common belief and its expression in the Liturgy. This is unity on the deepest of levels!

Lastly, it should be noted that even within each specific rite, such as the Latin Rite, various cultural traditions are often introduced. For example, the people of Mexico bring deep devotion to Our Lady of Guadalupe. This is seen especially in the way they celebrate her feast day on December 12. If you want a treat, try to attend this feast day celebration in a Catholic Church with a large Mexican population.

You will be inspired by their beautiful customs and devotion honoring Our Lady. Or, within the Filipino culture there is a tradition of celebrating nine consecutive Masses leading up to Christmas. This is called "Simbang Gabi." Often, excellent meals follow each Mass. We also see contemporary culture enter into the Liturgy at times in an appropriate way. For example, in the United States, contemporary Christian music is slowly becoming more common as an expression of our culture.

The bottom line is that diversity is good. And diversity on one level actually has the effect of helping us become more deeply united on the more important level of faith. We use different languages, different forms of music, differing devotions, various cultural emphases, and more to express our faith. But all those various expressions point to the same faith in the same God and it is this faith and worship of the one God that unites us as one in our various liturgical celebrations.

# 2

# THE SACRAMENTS: A PERSONAL ENCOUNTER

## Getting Personal!

The "Liturgy" in its broadest definition refers to every form of liturgical rite offered within the Church. This includes each of the Seven Sacraments, the Liturgy of the Hours, Benediction of the Blessed Sacrament, blessings, and various other forms of liturgical rites and celebrations.

Among all liturgical worship, the Sacraments take pride of place. Baptism is the gateway to the Sacraments and the Eucharist is the summit of the Sacraments. Each one offers the grace for a particular need.

Too often the Sacraments are seen primarily as an external ritual we participate in. They may be inspiring and uplifting, but some people never go beyond the externals. This is sad because the Sacraments are not meant to be only external signs and celebrations, they are also meant to be transforming internal realities in which we personally encounter the Living God! It is this deeply *personal* aspect that we will highlight here.

A sacrament is an action of Christ and the Church that brings about what it signifies. For example, the water poured at Baptism is both an external sign <u>and</u> a spiritual reality. In this sacrament, the external and visible sign of washing with water actually accomplishes the interior and spiritual reality of cleansing the soul from all sin, making the person a new creation. When this is understood and believed, the Sacraments are able to take full effect in our lives. We must comprehend what is taking place and allow the spiritual reality to touch and change our lives.

The proper attitude to have toward the celebration of the Sacraments is an attitude of personal union with God. We must realize that this is a heart to heart encounter in which we can be deeply transformed. If we fail to realize this, the Sacrament is still valid; however, we will not allow God to change us. It would be as if God showed up, spoke to us, invited us to let Him change our life, and we simply ignored Him. Our lack of personal participation does not change the fact that God showed up, but it does eliminate the possibility of receiving Him into our soul.

When celebrating any one of the Sacraments we must make it our goal to meet God in the depths of our being. It must be a real and transforming encounter with each person of the Trinity. We must look at the Sacraments with the spiritual eyes of faith: knowing, loving and receiving God Himself. This takes an authentic attitude of prayer.

There is a story of a child who came to realize this reality by watching his mother and father at Mass. This little child would follow them up to Holy Communion, return to the pew, and then watch as they closed their eyes and prayed. They tuned out everything else around them and entered into a deep communion with God. This child had been taught his catechism and understood that Holy Communion was the Body and Blood, Soul and Divinity of Christ. But it was this personal witness of his parents that truly taught the lesson of the Eucharist. Watching them encounter God in a real and personal way provided the insight necessary for him to want this sacred gift and to believe in the reality of the Eucharist. He understood, from the witness of his parents, that the Eucharist was real and deeply personal.

If the Sacraments were purely external, then fulfilling the external actions would suffice. But they are not just external; they are external and spiritual and require an interior spiritual participation. They require that one go through the external aspects, allow God to be made manifest, and then receive His presence and grace within one's soul. This is the way to celebrate the Sacraments!

It would be a very good idea if you spent time reflecting upon the way you celebrate the Sacraments. Do you meet God in a personal way? Do you truly pray the Sacraments? Are you letting God transform you as you participate? If you were to read this book in detail, knew all about the Sacraments and believed in what you study, this would not be enough. You must then live the Sacraments. They must become alive in your life. They must be true encounters with God and deeply personal encounters. Be honest with yourself. Think about your participation. And where your participation is lacking, resolve to make a change. You won't regret it! And you'll discover that these precious gifts actually can transform your life giving you all you need to live a fulfilled, holy and happy life!

**An Overview**

The Seven Sacraments are categorized as follows:
1. Sacraments of Initiation – Baptism, Confirmation, Eucharist
2. Sacraments of Healing – Confession, Anointing of the Sick
3. Sacraments at the Service of Communion – Marriage, Holy Orders

The following chapters will look at each of the Sacraments. We will reflect upon them not only from the theological and catechetical point of view (meaning the Church's teaching about them), but also from this very personal point of view. We have to discover how these sacraments can completely change our lives. We must understand that we meet God in each of them and that this encounter is deeply personal. So be open to looking at the Seven Sacraments in a whole new way!

**Three to Get In: Sacraments of Initiation**

The Sacraments of Christian initiation—Baptism, Confirmation, and the Eucharist—lay the *foundations* of every Christian life. "The sharing in the divine nature given to men through the grace of Christ bears a certain likeness to the origin, development, and nourishing of natural life. The faithful are born anew by Baptism, strengthened by the Sacrament of Confirmation, and receive in the Eucharist the food of eternal life. By means of these sacraments of

Christian initiation, they thus receive in increasing measure the treasures of the divine life and advance toward the perfection of charity" (Paul VI, apostolic constitution, Divinae consortium naturae: AAS 63 (1971) 657; cf. RCIA Introduction 1-2). (*CCC #1212*)

We're all familiar with initiation rites. For example, there are often rites of initiation for those college students who choose to join a fraternity or sorority. Or, when joining the military you have to go through basic training as a sort of initiation. When joining the Knights of Columbus in the Catholic Church, you must go through initiation ceremonies called degrees to become fully initiated.

In an analogous way, the Sacraments of Initiation are our official acts of initiation. But I say "in an analogous way" for a reason. The Sacraments are not just ceremonies or rituals you have to go through to be accepted as a member. They do not just symbolize our initiation nor are they a rite of passage. The Sacraments of Initiation actually *make* us members. They change us in such a way that we can never undo what is done. With these sacraments we are fully initiated. But initiated into what you may ask? They initiate us into two things: The Church and the Trinity. And these two are inseparable. To be initiated into one means you are initiated into the other. You can't have one, and not have the other.

Each sacrament will be dealt with in detail in the coming chapters, but for now let's look at the three Sacraments of Initiation together so as to see their unity and the unique focus of each. Each one of these sacraments involves the entire Trinity. But each one offers a unique personal focus also.

**Baptism:** Baptism makes us adopted sons and daughters of God. This is done by the power of the Holy Spirit and we are made new creations in Christ Jesus. But the unique focus offered here is the relationship that is established with the Father through baptism.

In baptism we receive a spiritual adoption. This is far more significant than a physical adoption. Spiritual adoption makes us true sons and daughters for eternity. We forever are given God as our Father. And the relationship with the Father becomes deeply personal. So the personal aspect we are invited to focus on is that, because of your baptism, you have a new relationship with God as your Father. This relationship is established so that you can enjoy all the fruits of being God's child. It means the Father knows you and you come to know the Father. It means that the relationship established is unbreakable and familial. It means you belong to God as you take on a new identity as God's child. This is who you are!

Baptism is not just a onetime event. Rather, it's a onetime event that has perpetual effects in our lives if we let it. It provides us with a permanent and unchanging relationship with God. Therefore, it is good to reflect daily upon your relationship with the Father that was established through baptism. Baptism has this ongoing effect in your life.

**Confirmation:** It should be obvious that confirmation provides us with a unique opportunity to deepen our personal relationship with the Holy Spirit. The Holy Spirit is not just some spiritual power of God, rather, the Holy Spirit is a Person: a divine Person we are called to know and love. Baptism introduces us to the Holy Spirit but it is confirmation that deepens our ability to have a true and transformative relationship with the Spirit. Confirmation is a sacrament in which the Holy Spirit enters our lives in a full way. We meet Him, get to know Him, and receive the unlimited benefits of that real and personal relationship. Knowing the Holy Spirit changes us. This relationship enables the Holy Spirit to possess us and act in and through us. We become one with Him in the Sacrament.

If you are confirmed, it is good to regularly reflect upon your daily conversation and relationship with God the Holy Spirit. Do you see Him active in your life? Is your relationship with Him guiding all your actions? Is He with you every moment of your day? God the Holy Spirit wants to have a friendship with you that is real and lasting. Once confirmed, He pledges to be there always as long as you remain open. Make the choice to be open and allow this friendship to change you.

**Eucharist:** The Eucharist is the Body, Blood, Soul and Divinity of Christ Jesus. Therefore, receiving the Eucharist has the unique effect of deepening our relationship with God the Son. It's easier to see God the Son in a personal way since He took on flesh in the Person of Jesus. Therefore, we should strive to see the Holy Eucharist as a calling to strengthen our personal bond with Him. The Eucharist is not just some spiritual food; rather, the Eucharist is God Himself entering our soul in a real and personal way. It is an invitation from God the Son to enter into communion with us. Receiving the Eucharist in faith transforms us into Him whom we consume. In a sense, it's right to say that we are consumed by Him whom we consume. And this consumption takes the form of a real and personal relationship.

It's also good to adore Christ in the Blessed Sacrament on a regular basis. Though receiving Him in Holy Communion is the ultimate goal, adoration of Him in the Blessed Sacrament prepares our soul to receive Him more deeply and helps us make our reception of Him more personal and more transforming.

It would be like preparing a meal. If someone sits and watches a gourmet meal being prepared all day, salivates over it, and looks forward to that first bite, then that first bite will be wonderful! In fact, the person who watches the meal be prepared, and anticipates eating it, will most likely enjoy it much more than the person who shows up at the last minute and consumes it quickly.

So it is with the Eucharist, if we take time to adore Christ, speak to Him, gaze upon Him and grow in a desire for Him, then our reception of Him in Holy Communion will be all the more fruitful.

**Trinity:** The Sacraments of Initiation have the effect of deepening our relationship with each person of the Holy Trinity. We become children of the Father in baptism, strengthened in our Christian walk by our deepened relationship with the Holy Spirit in Confirmation, and become one with Christ Jesus as we consume Him and adore Him in the Holy Eucharist. Therefore, the Sacraments of Initiation have the effect of introducing us into the full life of the Most Holy Trinity!

## Two to Heal: Sacraments of Healing

Despite the unlimited grace given through our personal relationship with the Trinity in the Sacraments of Initiation, we still sin and we still encounter sickness and death. For that reason, God comes to us with healing in two additional and unique ways.

**Confession:** The Sacrament of Confession, Penance, or Reconciliation offers us a unique encounter with God in our sinfulness. God loves us so much that He came to reconcile us with Himself. And He did it knowing full well that we are sinners in need of forgiveness and mercy.

Confession is an opportunity for a real and personal encounter with God in the midst of our sin. It's God's way of saying to us that He, personally, wants to tell us He forgives us. When we confess our sins and receive absolution we should see that this is an act of a personal God coming to us, hearing our sins, wiping them away and then telling us to go and sin no more.

So when you go to confession, make sure you see it as a personal encounter with our merciful God. Make sure you hear Him speak to you and know that it is God who enters your soul wiping your sin away.

**Anointing of the Sick:** God has a special care and concern for the weak, the sick, the suffering and the dying. We are not alone in these moments. In this sacrament we must strive to see this personal God come to us in compassion to care for us. We need to hear Him tell us He is near. We need to let Him transform our suffering, to bring the healing He desires (especially spiritual healing), and when our time comes, to let Him fully prepare our soul to meet Him in Heaven.

If you find yourself in need of this sacrament, make sure you look at it as this personal God coming to you in your time of need to offer you strength, mercy and compassion. Jesus knows what suffering and death are all about. He lived them. And He wants to be there for you in these moments.


**Two for the Mission: Sacraments of Vocation**

Each of us is given a mission. We are individually given a mission, and the Church as a whole is given a mission. The Sacraments of

Vocation are given to us so that we as individuals, and we as a Church, can live out the mission God has entrusted to us.

**Marriage**: The first mission God gave to Adam and Eve, as the first members of the human race, was to "become one" and then to "go forth and multiply." He established married life from the moment of creation as an integral part of humanity. Of course, the fall from the Garden of Eden left humanity so wounded that the perfect fulfillment of their mission became impossible. Therefore, God elevates this natural mission to a supernatural mission by establishing marriage as a sacrament. As a sacrament, marriage now includes a third participant. God now commits Himself to the couple in the form of a covenant. He enables each person in marriage to come to know, love and serve God Himself through coming to know, love and serve each other. Spouses love God as they love each other. Parents love God as they love their children. And parents, in addition, are enabled to be unique instruments of God in the lives of their children. All of this means that marriage is a divine gift which has the potential of fostering a personal communion with God through one another.

**Holy Orders:** Jesus wanted to remain with us always. He does this through prayer and the Sacraments. Another way He does this is through the ordained ministry. First, the ordained minister, a bishop priest or deacon, is given the privilege of being deeply united with God, communicating God to the world in his very person. God lives in the soul of the minister in a real and personal way. So the very act of exercising his ordained ministry has the effect of establishing a unique and personal relationship between God and the minister.

Holy Orders also enables all of God's people to encounter Him through His minister. This is especially the case in the ministry of the Sacraments. Ordination also allows God's people to meet Him personally through the minister's preaching and shepherding. And the more a minister is open to divine grace, the better an instrument he becomes of the very person of God.

Hopefully this brief overview of the Sacraments helps you come to understand the personal nature of God and the personal way He desires to come to us in the Sacraments. From here, let's look more deeply at each one of these sacred gifts.

# 3

# BAPTISM

> Holy Baptism is the basis of the whole Christian life, the gateway to life in the Spirit (*vitae spiritualis ianua*) (Council of Florence: DS 1314: vitae spiritualis ianua), and the door which gives access to the other Sacraments. (*CCC* #1213)

The word "baptism" means to "plunge" or "immerse." This plunging does something beyond description. It actually brings about a complete transformation of the person baptized. They are "born again." Remember what Jesus said to the Pharisee Nicodemus: "No one can enter the kingdom of God without being born of water and Spirit" (John 3:5). Baptism is that new birth. And this is not simply some symbolic or inspiring statement. Jesus is not just speaking in an analogous way. He's telling the truth! Baptism is an actual new birth by water and the Holy Spirit. And the result of this new birth is that a new person emerges. The old person enters into the water of baptism and dies. Then the new person rises from those waters. For this reason the ideal form of baptism is full immersion. The person is completely plunged into the water just as Jesus died and entered into the tomb. And then, just as Jesus rose from the tomb, so also the newly created Christian rises from the waters.

## Effects of Baptism

The fact that water is used for baptism signifies that there is a true cleansing that takes place. It's a washing away of sin and death. And since baptism is a sacrament, it accomplishes that which it signifies. In other words, it actually does wash away all sin and death.

**Original Sin:** First of all, *baptism washes away original sin.* When we were conceived in our mother's womb we were conceived in a state of original sin. This means we were conceived and born into the world in a state of 100% need. Our human nature is wounded to the point that we cannot achieve happiness without some essential help. We cannot make it to Heaven or union with God without some essential gift from God. This gift is what we call grace. And without grace we are doomed to sin and death. But God did not leave us abandoned. He did not leave us in our sin. His death and resurrection destroyed death itself and restored life. But the key question to ask here is this: How does God impart to us the grace that He won by His death and resurrection? How do we receive what He offered our fallen human nature? The answer, first and foremost, is Baptism!

Baptism is the first action in our lives that truly gives us grace. It is the doorway through which we enter the life of grace, become members of the Church, and share in the life of the Trinity. As the waters of Baptism are poured upon us, we are transformed by the life, death and resurrection of Jesus.

**Personal Sin:** When an adult is baptized, baptism also washes away all personal sins committed. Yes, we all sin. Therefore, those who are old enough to sin (those who have reached the age of reason), carry more than original sin, they also carry personal sins. But baptism is so transformative and complete that, when an adult is baptized, each and every personal sin they have committed is washed away. In the early Church there were even some who chose to wait to be baptized until they were older so that every sin would be washed away in this sacrament just before death. This early Christian practice misses the fact of God's ongoing mercy and forgiveness, but it illustrates the point that all personal sin is washed away. This is often received as very good news by those adults who are baptized after a checkered past. It's received as good news because, when they are baptized, all their sins are wiped away! What a grace!

**Indelible Spiritual Mark:** Baptism also places what we call an "indelible spiritual mark" on our soul. We're like animals who get branded. The physical mark is a permanent sign of who that animal's owner is. Similarly, in baptism our souls are marked with a permanent spiritual marking to reveal the fact that we forever remain children of God. Even if we seriously sin, this marking remains a constant source of grace calling us back to God.

**Children of God:** Baptism makes us adopted children of God. When we are baptized we enter into the new family of the Trinity. We become one with Christ Jesus, are filled with the Holy Spirit and are made children of the Father in Heaven. It is the unity with Jesus that brings this about. Since baptism has the effect of making us members of the Body of Christ, we are automatically filled with the Holy Spirit as a result. And when the Father looks at His Son Jesus, He also sees us as a member of His Son's body. Therefore, we can now call God our Father.

**New Brothers and Sisters:** If God is my Father, and God is your Father, then we share a new spiritual kinship. We are all brothers and sisters in Christ sharing the same Father in Heaven. So baptism brings about a spiritual unity and a spiritual family bond that cannot be lost. Once baptized, we will always share in this grace. Even if we become like wayward children, our Father is always waiting to welcome us back into His family by grace.

## Old Testament Prefigurations

Baptism was seen in a veiled way from the beginning of time. The fact that God would save us one day through water is also seen in the many ways that God saved His people in the Old Testament. Let's look at those ways.

**Creation:** The second sentence of the book of Genesis says there was "a mighty wind sweeping over the waters" (Genesis 1:2). This is a reference to the Holy Spirit breathing on the waters of creation making them a source of holiness for the world. This is the first baptismal image we have in the Scriptures.

**Noah:** God first chose to destroy the sinful world with water. This was a sign of baptism. Just as the waters covered the Earth and destroyed all things, so also baptism covers us and destroys sin. Noah and his family are the new humanity. So also we are part of that new humanity since washed with the waters of baptism.

**Red Sea:** The Red Sea is the most notable sign of baptism in the Old Testament. In this event we see God's people saved as they walk through the waters of this sea. As they pass through the waters, evil is destroyed behind them symbolized by the covering of Pharaoh's army with water. Yet the Israelites are led into freedom through these same waters.

**Jordan River:** On the final journey into the promised land, Joshua led the Israelites through the waters of the Jordan River. It was a mighty river but as soon as the priests carrying the Ark of the Covenant entered the waters, the river stopped flowing and the Israelites were able to pass through. This points to Baptism as the gateway to the promised land of grace in our lives.

## Giving Us This Sacrament

The Sacrament of Baptism was immediately presented to us when Jesus was baptized in the Jordan. John had been baptizing people and calling them to repentance. He was preparing them for the coming of the Messiah. And then Jesus the Son of God showed up to be baptized by John. John didn't want to do it at first but Jesus insisted. So He entered the Jordan and was baptized by John.

Did Jesus need this baptism? Did He need to repent? Obviously not. What Jesus did in that baptism could be called a "reverse baptism." In other words, as Jesus entered the water He Himself baptized the water. And by entering into the water He made all water holy and transmitted His grace to it so that it could henceforth be used as the instrument of the baptism of others.

Though Jesus was not changed by His baptism as we are, it was the beginning of His public ministry and the first manifestation of who He was. The Spirit descended in manifest form and the Father spoke from Heaven. This is a revelation of Jesus as a member of the Trinity sent by the Father and empowered by the Spirit to fulfill His divine mission of salvation.

Baptism, as a sacrament, was formally instituted by Jesus just before He ascended into Heaven. He said to His Apostles, "Go, therefore, and make disciples of all nations, baptizing them in the name of the Father, and of the Son, and of the Holy Spirit" (Matthew 28:19). With this command we have the glorious gateway to grace that Jesus intended.

## Who Baptizes Whom?

Baptism was entrusted to the Apostles by Jesus. He commanded them to go forth and baptize. Therefore, it is first and foremost the responsibility of bishops and priests to carry out this duty. Deacons are also ordinary ministers of Baptism since they share in the Sacrament of Holy Orders. But since Baptism is necessary for salvation and is intended for all people, it is possible for anyone to baptize. Here are a couple of examples to illustrate.

Imagine a child is born and the doctor says this child only has minutes to live. It would be proper for a parent to take water and baptize. This is done by three acts: 1) Pour water on the child's head; 2) Say, "I baptize you in the name of the Father, and of the Son and of the Holy Spirit; 3) Intend to baptize as the Church intends. So water, words and intention are all required.

This same child could actually be baptized by the doctor or nurse even if, for example, the doctor or nurse were Jewish or atheist. As long as the person baptizing fulfills the three requirements above, the child is truly baptized.

Something additional is required of those to be baptized who have reached the age of reason. They must desire Baptism and choose it for themselves, whereas infants are baptized when the parents alone intend to raise them in the faith of the Church. This poses an interesting question.

Is it better for a child to become an adult and then freely choose Baptism or is it better to baptize someone as a child? Of course our Church teaches it's best to baptize children rather than adults but the reasoning is important to understand.

Some will argue that it's better not to baptize as children because they need to make their own decision about their faith when they grow up. Children cannot choose Baptism or Christ. But our Church has the tradition of baptizing children. We do so because we believe it's better for a child to be raised in the faith. This presupposes they will choose Christ as they grow and mature and affords them all the grace they need to make this essential choice throughout their lives. So they still must make the choice to follow Christ as they grow and mature, but infant baptism helps them make the right choice. And even a two year old needs grace to begin learning right from wrong. So Baptism gives them what they need as they need it.

Now what about those who are not baptized you ask? What happens to them? And what about children who are not baptized? Are they doomed?

These questions can only be understood if we understand the perfect love and wisdom of God in all things. God is not legalistic. He does not look at a child who dies and say, "well, sorry but I only take baptized children into Heaven." This would be contrary to the infinite mercy and wisdom of God. Yet at the same time, the Church teaches that Baptism is the only way we know of that leads to salvation. Therefore, it is necessary. So how do we reconcile these views that appear to be opposed? That is, how do we reconcile a loving God with the teaching that Baptism is necessary for salvation?

This is done quite easily. We believe that Baptism is the only way we know of (the only way God revealed to us) to receive the grace of salvation. But God, in His infinite love and wisdom is not constrained or bound by the limited revelation He shared with us. God can do whatever He wants to do. We are bound by the Sacraments but God is not. Therefore, if a child dies before Baptism, the parents should rest assured that God loves that child far more than they do. And this perfectly loving God will act in a way that is perfectly loving toward that child. One speculation is that God offers that child the same choice He offered the angels. They had a onetime opportunity to choose. So it is entirely possible that when this child dies and faces God, this child will be invited to choose to love God freely and, thus, spend eternity with God. But we must always remember that Heaven does require a free choice. Therefore, not even a child would be forced to be there against his or her will.

Another interesting scenario is the adult who is not baptized. What happens when that adult dies? Again, we must look at this from the point of view of a God who is infinitely wise and infinitely loving. In this case there are a few possibilities. The first possibility is what is referred to as "baptism by blood." This would be the person who desires Baptism but, before actually receiving this sacrament, is martyred for his faith. We don't see this that often today but it was a real situation in the early Church. We believe that this desire to be baptized, as well as the act of martyrdom, earn the grace of Baptism by means other than water and thus the person receives all the graces and effects of a traditional baptism.

Similarly, we speak of "baptism by desire." This would include those who believe and desire Baptism but die before they are baptized by water. Again, the desire alone suffices for God to pour forth His grace. This would also apply to children who die before they are baptized when the parents desired Baptism. The desire on the part of the parents suffices for the grace to be poured forth.

Lastly, we need to look at the situation of those who did not choose to be baptized and, therefore, died without this sacrament. These cases will fall in one of two categories. First, there are those who *through no fault of their own* did not come to an explicit faith in Christ and, as a result, did not seek Baptism. In this case God will judge only the heart. There are many reasons why a person may not come to explicit faith in Christ through no fault of their own. Say, for example, that a person lives in some culture where the Gospel has never been preached and they actually have never heard of Jesus. Does God consider them to be deserving of eternal damnation because they never had the opportunity to hear about Jesus? Certainly not.

Another example would be the person who heard about Jesus but received only a message of hypocrisy. Let's say that the message preached was continually skewed and malicious. Perhaps the preacher was living a double life and the person hearing about Jesus rejected the explicit Gospel message because of this messenger. Furthermore, we should presume that the Gospel message was being presented in a very disordered way. In that case, the rejection of the message may actually have been a rejection of the hypocrisy of the messenger. And that may be a good thing!

The bottom line is that God knows the heart and God sees the intention in that heart. So if someone fails to come to an explicit faith in Christ and, therefore, fails to receive the Sacrament of Baptism in an explicit way, God will still look only at the heart. And when He does look into that heart, if He sees goodness and faith, He will pour out His grace anyway. So, a person who is not baptized may actually be following the voice of God in their conscience without even realizing whose voice it is. In reality, this person has faith and God will see that!

The only case that may end with eternal damnation is the person who fails to receive Baptism through their own fault. They are given every opportunity to hear the Gospel, they have the good Christian witness of others, and they interiorly reject this of their own free will. Free will is the key here. And, again, only God knows the heart and only God can be the judge of one's heart. So if God sees in the heart an obstinacy that is freely chosen, then this person is guilty and may lose that offer of eternal salvation. This is sad.

## The Celebration of Baptism

Baptism is celebrated according to a set liturgical rite that has evolved over the centuries. A detailed explanation would be a book in itself. For our purposes, we will look only at some of the essential parts of the liturgical rite and speak to their symbolism and meaning. This reflection is based on the Rite of Baptism for Children but the symbolism and meaning applies to adults who are baptized also.

**Beginning at the Entrance of the Church:** Baptism begins at the entrance of the Church. This is done as a symbolic gesture of what is happening. The child being baptized is being welcomed into the Church as a member of Christ's body. The church building is a symbol of Christ's spiritual Body, the Church. Therefore, the person is met at the entrance and welcomed into Christ Jesus.

**Marked with the Sign of the Cross:** The person to be baptized is then marked on the forehead with the sign of the Cross by the minister, the parents and the godparents. This symbolic gesture is an indication of what is soon to take place. The child will be marked by Baptism with an indelible spiritual marking from God on their soul.

**Proclamation of the Scriptures:** The Word of God is read and a homily is given. This shows that faith comes through hearing the Word of God. And the response to that faith is first and foremost Baptism.

**Anointing with Oil of Catechumen:** A prayer against evil is prayed over the child (a prayer of exorcism), and then the child is anointed with oil that was previously blessed by the bishop. This prayer acknowledges the reality of evil in our world and, at the beginning of the child's Christian life, offers the grace of protection. The child is then anointed on the breast as a sign of receiving a breastplate of protection.

**Blessing of Water:** The minister moves to the baptismal font and prays a prayer of blessing upon the water. The most traditional of prayers used is one which recounts the history of God's use of water. It recounts the events mentioned earlier in this chapter regarding the following: The Spirit breathed on the waters at Creation; the story of Noah; The Red Sea; The Jordan; and the Baptism of Jesus.

**Renunciation of Sin and Profession of Faith:** The parents and godparents are asked to profess their faith and, in so doing, to profess the faith in which the child is about to be baptized. In this profession of faith, they are promising to raise the child in this faith they profess.

**Rite of Baptism:** The essential part of Baptism is the pouring, sprinkling or immersion with water. While the water touches the person the Trinitarian formula is said: "I baptize you in the name of the Father, and of the Son, and of the Holy Spirit." The minister must also have the intention to do what the Church intends to do, namely, to baptize.

**Chrism:** Chrism is a mixture of oil and perfume. It is blessed by the bishop at a special Mass during Holy Week called the Chrism Mass. This chrism is also used in Confirmation and Holy Orders. The oil is a symbol of the anointing of the Holy Spirit and the perfume is a symbol of the sweet fragrance of Christ which must always permeate their lives.

**Baptismal Garment:** The child is covered with a white garment which is a symbol of being clothed in Christ. White is a symbol of purity and freedom from sin.

**Candle:** The parents and godparents then receive a lit candle. The candle is lit from the Easter candle which is a symbol of Christ Himself. The light is entrusted to the parents and godparents as a way of telling them they are now responsible to keep this light of faith alive in the heart of this child through their words and actions so that the faith given in Baptism will reach culmination one day in Heaven.

**Blessing of Parents:** The rite concludes with a special blessing of the parents. This blessing acknowledges the fact that parents play an essential role in the Christian upbringing and formation of children who are baptized. They can only fulfill this role with the help of God!

# 4

# THE SACRAMENT OF CONFIRMATION

It must be explained to the faithful that the reception of the Sacrament of Confirmation is necessary for the completion of baptismal grace (Roman Ritual, Rite of Confirmation (OC), Introduction 1). For "by the Sacrament of Confirmation, [the baptized] are more perfectly bound to the Church and are enriched with a special strength of the Holy Spirit. Hence they are, as true witnesses of Christ, more strictly obliged to spread and defend the faith by word and deed" (LG 11; cf. OC, Introduction 2). (*Catechism* #1285)

So what is the Sacrament of Confirmation all about? Is it just a nice maturity ritual within the Catholic Church? Is it simply your own adult decision to be Catholic? Is it your graduation ceremony from religious education classes?!? No, it's not any of these.

Confirmation can be confusing at times. Perhaps the name itself can be misleading. It is thought, at times, that Confirmation is my opportunity to "confirm" my faith. Well, yes, you certainly must do this as you receive this sacrament. But this does not get at the heart of Confirmation. Confirmation is not so much about *you* confirming your choice to be Catholic; rather, it's about *God* the Holy Spirit confirming you! It's much more something that God does to you and your eternal soul than something you do for God or even yourself.

Like Baptism, Confirmation changes your soul. You receive a spiritual character (an indelible mark) on your soul. And this marking becomes a permanent source of grace for you throughout eternity. It's God's way of making a permanent commitment to you by deepening His covenant commitment made to you at Baptism. In other words, at Baptism God said to you, "you are my son" "you are my daughter." And now that you have grown and matured in your faith God now says, "I am deepening my bond with you and empowering you to live out your baptismal calling to a greater degree." God knows we need help to live out our baptismal dignity and calling. He knows we cannot do it by ourselves. Therefore, He gives us the fullness of the Holy Spirit in Confirmation so as to provide all we need to live as we are called. What a grace!

To understand this precious and life-changing gift from God, let's begin with an understanding of the promise of the Holy Spirit in the Scriptures as well as the institution of this sacrament in those same Scriptures. Don't skip this section! A good scriptural understanding of the Holy Spirit will add much insight into the living out of your Christian faith by the power of the Holy Spirit.

### What Scripture Reveals

Scripture reveals this wondrous gift of Confirmation in many ways. It's seen in a veiled way in the Old Testament, promised by Jesus in the Gospels, and made fully manifest in the Acts of the Apostles. Below are some Scriptural references to Confirmation. They help set a good foundation for our understanding of this sacrament.

**Isaiah:** Isaiah 11:2 speaks of the Holy Spirit resting upon the promised Messiah. This is Jesus, the Son of God. He will be filled with the Holy Spirit and, as a result, will manifest in His very person all the glorious gifts of the Holy Spirit.

> The spirit of the LORD shall rest upon him: a spirit of wisdom and of understanding, a spirit of counsel and of strength, a spirit of knowledge and of fear of the LORD...

Isaiah 61:1-3 says the following:

> The spirit of the Lord GOD is upon me, because the LORD has anointed me; he has sent me to bring good news to the afflicted, to bind up the brokenhearted, to proclaim liberty to the captives, release to the prisoners, to announce a year of favor from the LORD and a day of vindication by our God; To comfort all who mourn; to place on those who mourn in Zion, a diadem instead of ashes, to give them oil of gladness instead of mourning, a glorious mantle instead of a faint spirit.

Both of these passages reveal that the Messiah will be filled with the Holy Spirit. These passages also reveal the effects of the Holy Spirit. Jesus certainly lived these perfectly since He was perfectly one with the Holy Spirit. But for our purposes in reflecting upon the Sacrament of Confirmation, we should see these gifts and effects of the Holy Spirit in the life of the Messiah as invitations to each of us to also receive these same gifts and these same effects. We are to be Christ to the world and, thus, allow the Holy Spirit to act in us in the same way the Spirit acted in Jesus. This fact is seen in the following passage from the prophet Ezekiel:

> I will put my spirit within you so that you walk in my statutes, observe my ordinances, and keep them. (Ezekiel 36:27)

**Gospels:** Mathew 3:16 and John 1:32-33, both speak of the baptism of Jesus. At that baptism we read that the Holy Spirit descended upon Jesus in the form of a dove. It's true that the Holy Spirit was already fully alive in Jesus' life, so, truth be told, Jesus did not receive the Holy Spirit at this moment. He was already one with the Spirit and the Father. This manifestation of the Holy Spirit upon Jesus at His baptism took place so that all of us would witness the manifestation of this unity through the eyes of faith. It was a physical and historical manifestation of what was already there.

This episode took place, in part, to reveal to us that there is a Holy Spirit waiting to descend upon us also. Such an outpouring takes place in Baptism, but it also takes place through the unique and total outpouring of the Holy Spirit in the Sacrament of Confirmation. Jesus' witness reveals our own calling in the Sacrament of Confirmation.

The fact that we are all called to receive the Holy Spirit is also made clear in the Gospels. Here are a few passages that reveal this sacred fact:

> For the Holy Spirit will teach you at that moment what you should say. (Luke 12:12)

> Whoever believes in me, as scripture says: "Rivers of living water will flow from within him." He said this in reference to the Spirit that those who came to believe in him were to receive. There

was, of course, no Spirit yet, because Jesus had not yet been glorified. (John 7:38-39)

But I tell you the truth, it is better for you that I go. For if I do not go, the Advocate will not come to you. But if I go, I will send him to you. (John 16:7)

**Acts of the Apostles:** The Acts of the Apostles records the activity within the early Church after Jesus ascended into Heaven. This is the KEY to understanding the actual Sacrament of Confirmation. Up until this point we see many promises of the Holy Spirit and we find, in the Old Testament and in Jesus' own words, many insights into the effect of the Holy Spirit. But here, in the Acts, we see these promises being fulfilled. We actually see the Spirit descending upon humanity and working wonders in the lives of those receiving the Holy Spirit. This takes place at Pentecost and is recorded in Acts 2:1-4:

When the time for Pentecost was fulfilled, they were all in one place together. And suddenly there came from the sky a noise like a strong driving wind, and it filled the entire house in which they were. Then there appeared to them tongues as of fire, which parted and came to rest on each one of them. And they were all filled with the Holy Spirit and began to speak in different tongues, as the Spirit enabled them to proclaim.

Immediately after being filled with the Holy Spirit, the Apostles went out into the streets and began to proclaim the Gospel of Jesus with boldness and confidence. And another amazing thing happened. They were also given the gift of tongues! With this gift they spoke the Gospel in their language but, miraculously, all who were gathered heard them speak in their own native language. A close reading of this Scripture reveals that the Apostles were heard in at least fifteen different languages. Of course, everyone was confused and was wondering how this had happened.

At that, Peter stood up and revealed that it was a fulfillment of the Prophet Joel who said:

"It will come to pass in the last days," God says, "that I will pour out a portion of my spirit upon all flesh. Your sons and your daughters shall prophesy, your young men shall see visions, your old men shall dream dreams. Indeed, upon my servants and my handmaids I will pour out a portion of my spirit in those days, and they shall prophesy. And I will work wonders in the heavens above and signs on the earth below: blood, fire, and a cloud of smoke. The sun shall be turned to darkness, and the moon to blood, before the coming of the great and splendid day of the Lord, and it shall be that everyone shall be saved who calls on the name of the Lord." (Acts 2:17-21)

Peter then went on to proclaim the truth about Jesus to all who were there. He spoke of the fact that Jesus was the Messiah who came into the world from the Father, suffered, died, was buried and rose on the third day. Peter then called everyone to repentance for the forgiveness of sins. And even though there were some who were deeply confused and even angered at Peter for speaking these truths, he did not back down because he was now empowered by the Holy Spirit.

One of the best ways to understand the effects of the Holy Spirit as given in the Sacrament of Confirmation is to read the entire book of the Acts of the Apostles. Look especially at the fear and timidity the Apostles experienced before Pentecost. They were afraid of being arrested and persecuted and suffering the same fate as Jesus on the Cross. But after Pentecost (Confirmation) they were suddenly bold and filled with incredible gifts and charisms and became powerful instruments of the Gospel. They were now able to carry out the mission they were given by Jesus.

The same is true for us. We may want to fulfill our Christian calling, but all too often we are afraid. Let's face it. We are often afraid to let our faith in Christ move from our heart to our mouths and actions. There is often a fear that paralyzes us and keeps us from confidently and openly allowing our faith to be made manifest for all to see.

Take, for example, the fact that so many are embarrassed to make the sign of the Cross and say grace before their meal in a restaurant or in any other public setting. Or the fact that it's hard to post something about our faith on Facebook or other social media. We are often afraid to speak of our love of Christ and to practice our faith openly in our social circles.

Why is this? It's because the Gift of God, the Gift of the Holy Spirit has not taken hold. Even if we have received the Sacrament of Confirmation we can still be timid. This tells us that we must open ourselves up all the more to let the effects of the Holy Spirit become active in our lives. Fear must be cast out and confidence must take its place.

Perhaps the best way to start down this road is to understand, more fully, the actual effects of the Holy Spirit in the Sacrament of Confirmation. With a proper understanding of these effects we can more easily allow the Holy Spirit to do what He wants to do. So let's look at what He wants to do.

## Effects of Confirmation

You could say that the Apostles didn't see what hit them. They didn't see it coming. But when it came, they ran with it. What is this "it?" "It" is the Person of the Holy Spirit made fully present in the Sacrament of Confirmation. Once the Holy Spirit descended upon them at Pentecost, they were totally changed. This is clearly seen in their actions. They were now bold, insightful, filled with wisdom and knowledge, charismatic, and focused upon fulfilling the mission given them by the Father. This was a new and exciting journey in their lives made possible only by the power of the Holy Spirit fully alive within them.

To understand the way God wants to transform you by the Sacrament of Confirmation let's look at the effects of Confirmation as outlined in the *Catechism* #1303:

> —it roots us more deeply in the divine filiation which makes us cry,
>     "Abba! Father!"; (Rom 8:15)
> —it unites us more firmly to Christ;
> —it increases the gifts of the Holy Spirit in us;
> —it renders our bond with the Church more perfect; (LG 11)
> —it gives us a special strength of the Holy Spirit to spread and
>     defend the faith by word and action as true witnesses of Christ,

to confess the name of Christ boldly, and never to be ashamed of the Cross: (Council of Florence (1439): DS 1319; LG 11; 12)

Now before your eyes glaze over, let's try to discover what these effects actually mean for you in your personal journey of faith. Let's see how these effects are, in fact, extraordinarily exciting for your daily life!

**It roots us more deeply in the divine filiation which makes us cry, "Abba! Father!":** This statement of faith may go right over your head at first, but let's look at it this way. Do you want to belong? Do you want to be loved, accepted, cared for and cherished? Do you want to be part of a family that is exceptionally close and supportive? Do you want parents who love you unconditionally and are always there for you? Do you want to love and be loved? Do you want to know others and to be known? Do you want to understand others and to be understood?

Any honest person would recognize within themselves these desires. The answer would be a profound and sincere "yes" to all of the above. Why? Because this is what it means to be human! It's what we are made for.

"Divine filiation" simply means that Confirmation deepens our bond with God the Father. At baptism, we are made sons and daughters of God. But Confirmation strengthens that bond in that it enables us to "cry, 'Abba Father!'" This is interesting and it takes a bit of insight to properly understand. Confirmation does not make God the Father love us any more than He already does. That would be impossible. It does not mean that we now become even more of a son or daughter of God. Rather, it has to do with *our* new found ability to *cry out* that God is our Father! It means that Confirmation enables us to realize this gift, given at Baptism, all the more! It not only enables us to realize we are a son or daughter, it also enables us to profess this reality with our whole being. It gives a new strength and zeal to claim God as our Father.

By analogy, it would be like a teenager who has a bad attitude toward his parents and thinks they don't understand him. This all-too-common feeling on the part of a teenager reveals that some teens do not yet understand the beautiful and profound gift of a parent. Now imagine that this same teen grows up, gets married and has a child of his own. In the act of becoming a parent, this onetime rebellious teen suddenly realizes what it means to also be a child. He starts to realize the love that a parent has, and he begins to realize the profound commitment made by a parent. As a result of being a parent himself, he begins to love his own parents all the more. His love and admiration for his own parents grow as his love for his own children increases.

Similarly, with Confirmation, we are given the grace to share the Gospel with others and, in a sense, nurture others in the faith as a parent nurtures a child. We are strengthened to be instruments of the divine love of the Father for others. And, in the exercise of this responsibility, we also begin to understand our own profound commitment and relationship to God as our Father. We discover more of what it means to be a son or daughter and this enables us to more deeply "cry out" to God with a profound and all-consuming love.

**It unites us more firmly to Christ:** The Eucharist, as we will see in the next chapter, unites us profoundly with Christ. In that sacrament we receive His very Body and Blood, Soul and Divinity! But Confirmation also unites us more firmly to Christ Jesus. Jesus and the Holy Spirit are one and they are both united to the Father in a perfect unity. So, if we are more intimately united to the Holy Spirit in Confirmation, and enabled to fully "cry out" that God is our Father, then the logical conclusion is that we are also more deeply united to God the Son. It's impossible to be more united with the Holy Spirit and not, at the same time, be more deeply united to the Son who is one with the Holy Spirit.

This is significant because the Son of God became man. He became a human in the person of Jesus. Jesus, therefore, is the perfection of human nature and is therefore the one who we are called to imitate as Christians. But we are called to do more than just imitate Jesus, we are called to be united with Him, to live in Him, to have Him live in us, and to be His very hands and feet, His mouth and heart, His entire body in the world. We are called to be Christ in this world and it is through the gift of the Holy Spirit that we are uniquely able to do just that to a more perfect degree. The Holy Spirit enables us to live out our mission of being transformed in Christ Jesus.

Yes, this happens in Baptism, but it is firmed up and strengthened in Confirmation. As the Holy Spirit descends upon us, we are, in a sense, "supercharged" to be more like Christ. Jesus had the perfection of the Gifts of the Holy Spirit. In Confirmation, we also are more fully perfected with these gifts enabling us to be more like Christ.

**It increases the gifts of the Holy Spirit in us:** The Gifts of the Holy Spirit enable us to fully live the Christian life. There are seven of these gifts which, together, offer us all we need to fully live the life of Christ. Below are these seven gifts. I'd encourage you to take them and reflect upon them prayerfully. They'd actually be a good source of prayer and meditation. They are also a good examination of conscience. As you ponder these Seven Gifts of the Holy Spirit, you are most certainly going to find that you have not perfected them. That's OK! Discovering where you are lacking in the Holy Spirit is the first step in deepening your bond with the Holy Spirit so that these gifts may increase.

The Gifts are broken up into two sections:

> **Helping me *know* God's will:**
> Wisdom, Understanding, Counsel, Knowledge

> **Helping me *do* God's will:**
> Fortitude, Reverence, Fear of the Lord

Here is a summary of each gift. Again, read them slowly and perhaps take them to prayer. If you have been confirmed, you can be certain that God wants to increase these Gifts in your life.

**Wisdom**...

> Helps you see life from God's point of view.
> Helps you see the real value of persons, events, things.
> Keeps you from foolishly judging by appearances.
> "Blessed are the peacemakers..." Seeing things from God's perspective brings harmony and peace!

## Understanding…

Helps you understand all the truths of God you've learned since childhood.
Jesus "opened their minds" to understand the Scriptures! (Luke 24:45)
This is more than just knowing what God says, it's about understanding deeply.
We can make sense of the most difficult experiences of life such as suffering.
"Blessed are the pure of heart, for they will see God…" We see and understand!

## Counsel…

Helps you seek advice and offer correct advice to others.
Helps you be open to the good advice of parents, teachers, peers, priests, friends, etc.
This gift also shows us we need others in our lives so as to make good decisions.
"Blessed are the merciful, they will be shown mercy…" Helping others also helps us!

## Knowledge…

Opinions are not always helpful, what we need is the truth.
Helps you know what God wants you to do in particular situations.
Helps you avoid the many temptations of the world by seeing them correctly.
"Blessed are the sorrowful, they will be consoled…" Sorrow helps us learn from past mistakes!

## Fortitude…

Also known as "Supernatural Courage" in matters of faith and morality.
Gives firmness of mind and will to do good and avoid evil.
Gives us well-founded hope of persevering through difficulties.
We have a new depth of patience, peace and joy through difficult situations.

"Blessed are those who hunger and thirst for righteousness..."
We will press on when life is hard!

## Reverence...

We have a deep reverence for God, the Mass, the Scriptures and all things pertaining to God.
We also have a new reverence for every person as an *"imago dei"* (Image of God).
Helps us revere life from conception to natural death.
Have a greater respect for elders, parents, country, legitimate authority.
We even love the sinner while despising sin.
"Blessed are those who hunger and thirst for righteousness..."
We love all that is good!

## Fear of the Lord...

We begin by loving God because we fear loss of Him and the sadness this causes.
We move deeper when our "fear" turns into a fear of offending God or others *out of love for them.* We become keenly aware of anything that may harm our relationship with God or others.
We even become aware of how attachments to earthly things can harm our relationships.
"Blessed are the poor in spirit..." We become detached from everything that is not important!

**It renders our bond with the Church more perfect:** The Church, as explained in detail in Book One of this series, is the Body of Christ. And if Confirmation more firmly unites us to Christ Jesus, then it is a logical conclusion that we are also more deeply united to the Church herself through the Sacrament of Confirmation. By becoming more like Christ, we become a fuller member of His Body, the Church. As a result, we are called to live out the mission of the Church in the unique way the Holy Spirit enables us.

In John's Gospel, Chapter 20:21-22, Jesus appeared to His Apostles inviting them to fulfill their unique mission by the power of the Holy Spirit.

Jesus said to them again, "Peace be with you. As the Father has sent me, so I send you." And when he had said this, he breathed on them and said to them, "Receive the Holy Spirit."

This was a particular call to the Apostles to share in the mission of Jesus' priesthood. But all of us should see in this Scripture Jesus' universal call to continue His very mission by the power of the Holy Spirit.

Confirmation makes us full members of the Church since we receive all we need to act as members of Christ's Body. We are His hands and feet and we have what we need to fulfill this high calling.

**It gives us a special strength of the Holy Spirit to spread and defend the faith by word and action as true witnesses of Christ, to confess the name of Christ boldly, and never to be ashamed of the Cross:** This last effect of Confirmation, spoken of in the *Catechism*, is seen in all of the above explanations. Specifically, it points out that our witnessing to the faith is done "by word and action," and that we are enabled to do this "boldly," and to "never be ashamed of the Cross."

This goes to the heart of our temptation toward fear. The world can be tough on Christians. We can feel like we stand out. We experience many sorts of persecutions and humiliations when we live our faith. We experience even more persecution and humiliations by the world when we boldly profess the truth by our words and actions.

Take, for example, the truths about human sexuality, marriage, and abortion. These truths of our faith are not popular in the world. And when we speak them with compassion and love, they are not always received that way. Many will attack these truths and, in so doing, will attack us as their messengers. We do need to be careful that when speaking truths that are hard for people to receive we do so only out of love and compassion. But, nonetheless, we should not be surprised if the world challenges and even attacks as we act as instruments of the Gospel. For that reason, we need the Holy Spirit. We need the grace, courage, boldness and love God gives so as to be able to carry out this mission to the world that so desperately needs the truth.

## Receiving the Sacrament of Confirmation

The Sacrament of Confirmation, being one of the Sacraments of Initiation, is intended to be given to every baptized Christian. In the Latin Rite of the Church, Confirmation can be given any time after the age of reason (about seven years old). Interestingly, the Eastern Catholic Church has the tradition of administering the Sacraments of Baptism, Confirmation and Eucharist together in infancy. This reveals the unity of these three Sacraments. The Latin Rite of the Church waits to offer Confirmation and Eucharist until the age of reason which emphasizes the free choice to receive these sacraments as well as the free choice to live out the Christian faith. Often times, particular dioceses or parishes will set the age of Confirmation even later such as middle school or high school. There are various reasons this is done, but what is important to know is that the universal law of the Latin Church allows for the reception of Confirmation any time after the age of reason and allows the various conferences of bishops in each country to decide on a more specific age. Many countries leave it up to the local bishop to decide the exact age of Confirmation in his diocese.

Another interesting fact is that, at least theologically speaking, it seems preferable to receive Confirmation prior to receiving the Eucharist. Though this does not always happen for more practical reasons, it is still the norm. The *Catechism*, for example, presents the teaching on Confirmation right after the section on Baptism and right before the section on the Eucharist.

Another practical thing to consider is the minister of Confirmation. Ideally, the bishop of the local diocese will be the one to administer this sacrament. Why? Because it symbolically emphasizes the bond that is established with the Church. The bishop is not only the chief shepherd of the local diocese, he is also the primary sign of the unity within that local church (diocese). Additionally, since the Sacrament of Confirmation offers the full outpouring of the Holy Spirit, it is appropriate that this sacrament be given by the one who has the fullness of the priesthood in the local church. And that is the bishop. However, for practical reasons, there are times when another priest is entrusted with the responsibility of Confirmation. This is done by delegation from the bishop and imparts the same grace imparted by the bishop.

Confirmation, like Baptism, is given once and only once. After it is given, the grace is always there. Even if someone is not fully open to the grace of this sacrament at the time of Confirmation, they can always open their hearts at a later time. It's as if the grace of this sacrament lays dormant in the soul waiting to be tapped into and experienced.

Lastly, there are a couple of profound signs and symbols that are used when the Sacrament of Confirmation is conferred.

## Signs and Symbols

**Chrism:** Chrism is a mixture of oil and fragrance. The oil is a sign of anointing, joy, healing, cleansing, beauty and strength. It symbolizes the anointing of the Holy Spirit and, in fact, brings about this spiritual anointing. The fragrance symbolizes the sweetness of Christ which must always permeate our lives. Others will come to know we are Christians simply by the fragrance of Christ's love that flows from us as a result of Confirmation.

Chrism is mixed and blessed by the bishop every year during Holy Week at the Chrism Mass. This is significant in that, even if the bishop is not able to be the one conferring the Sacrament of Confirmation in the parish, he is still present in that the oil used at Confirmation previously was consecrated by him.

**Laying on of Hands:** The bishop (or priest) who confers the Sacrament of Confirmation, places his hands on the head of the one to be confirmed. This action is a sign of the outpouring of the Holy Spirit. It's a bestowing of this grace from person to person, from the ordained minister acting in the Person of Christ, to the one receiving this full outpouring of the Holy Spirit.

**Character:** It's also important to understand that the Sacrament of Confirmation imparts a spiritual character, or seal, upon the one receiving this sacrament. This is also referred to as an "indelible mark." Though this marking, or seal, is not visible, it is symbolized by the anointing with the chrism upon the forehead with the sign of the Cross. During this anointing, the bishop (or priest) says, "Be sealed with the Gift of the Holy Spirit."

## The Bottom Line is the Upper Limit

Confirmation is the wondrous Gift that was promised in the Old Testament, reaffirmed by Jesus, and fulfilled after Jesus' Resurrection. This grace is offered to all. And to the extent that we open our hearts to this grace, this sacrament can change our lives!

The fact that God gave us this sacrament is proof that He wants all of the Gifts of the Holy Spirit alive within each of us. The goal is not to allow only some of the gifts to take hold partially; rather, the goal is to allow all of the gifts to take hold in a complete and total way. This is done when we allow ourselves to be drawn into a deep and *personal* relationship with the Holy Spirit.

Yes, let's not forget that the Holy Spirit is a Person! A divine Person. We are called to know and love the Holy Spirit. This can, at first, seem like a strange concept. It may seem strange because it's hard to think of one who is a pure spirit as a person. But we have to overcome any difficulties we have with accepting and embracing this relationship in a personal way.

Entering into a personal relationship with the Holy Spirit is the fundamental "bottom line" of our Christian walk. It must be done! Embracing this essential relationship will also bring us to the "upper limit" of our Christian calling. The Holy Spirit has great plans for us and will give us all we need to fulfill those plans of God.

Let's conclude with a beautiful prayer to the Holy Spirit. This is a prayer that could be said every day. It would especially be good to pray the first three words of this prayer over and over. You will be amazed at the effect this will have on your life if you commit yourself to this prayer every day and even throughout the day. Pray the entire prayer each morning and then, throughout the day, simply repeat the first three words: "Come Holy Spirit." Pray those words as you walk, as you drive, as you do chores and every time they come to mind. Saying them should become a regular habit of your soul. If you can establish this habit you will be amazed at how close you become with God the Holy Spirit!

> Come Holy Spirit, fill the Hearts of the faithful, enkindle in them the fire of Your love. Send forth Your Spirit and they shall be created. And You shall renew the face of the Earth.

> O, God, who by the light of the Holy Spirit, did instruct the hearts of the faithful, grant that by the same Holy Spirit we may be truly wise and ever enjoy His consolation, Through Christ our Lord, Amen.

# 5

## THE MOST HOLY EUCHARIST

> The holy Eucharist completes Christian initiation. Those who have been raised to the dignity of the royal priesthood by Baptism and configured more deeply to Christ by Confirmation participate with the whole community in the Lord's own sacrifice by means of the Eucharist. (*Catechism* #1322)

There are many things in this world that are truly priceless. You cannot put a price on the beauty of the mountains or other wonders of nature. You could never put a price on a parent's love or on the gift of a child. You cannot put a price on a faithful friend or a heroic act of charity. And you cannot put a price on the gift of the Most Holy Eucharist!

The Eucharist is an incredible mystery. It is, in fact, the mystery of all mysteries. St. Thomas Aquinas expressed the mystery and magnificence of the Eucharist in his famous chant, *Adoro te Devote*:

> Prostrate I adore Thee, Deity unseen,
> Who Thy glory hidest 'neath these shadows mean;
> Lo, to Thee surrendered, my whole heart is bowed,
> Tranced as it beholds Thee, shrined within the cloud.
>
> Taste, and touch, and vision, to discern Thee fail;
> Faith, that comes by hearing, pierces through the veil.
> I believe whate'er the Son of God hath told;
> What the Truth hath spoken, that for truth I hold.

The first two stanzas of that chant state that we should prostrate ourselves before the divine majesty of God who is hidden behind the veil of the Sacred Host. Our senses are deceived and we fail to perceive the reality present. It is only by the inspired gift of faith that we can come to see and believe in the True Presence. It is only by the grace of God that we can begin to comprehend the sublime mystery of the Most Holy Eucharist.

## Essence Challenges our Five Senses

The Eucharist, simply put, is God. The Eucharist is God the Son, fully present in our world. It is Jesus, the eternal Son of God, fully present. The Eucharist is His Body, Blood, Soul and Divinity.

God is made present to us in this form through the use of signs and symbols. But we should not fail to believe that the Eucharist is much more than signs and symbols. It could be said that the bread is a symbol of His Body and the wine is a symbol of His Blood. This is true, but it is also far from complete. We must follow up that statement by saying that the bread, a symbol of His Body, actually becomes His Body, and the wine, a symbol of His Blood, actually becomes His Blood. We call this Transubstantiation. That's a big word with a lot of meaning.

"Transubstantiation" means that the substance is transformed. It's changed. But it also means that the external aspects of the bread and wine remain the same. They do not change to our sight, taste, touch or smell. They look the same, feel the same and taste the same. But they are not the same in their essence.

Try to imagine two primary parts of a piece of bread and a glass of wine. There are the external aspects and the essence. The external aspects are all those perceptible by the senses. But the essence is not perceptible in any way.

By analogy, it could be like closing your eyes and smelling a rose-scented perfume. Your nose tells you that a rose is before you, but, in reality, it is a manufactured fragrance. Your nose is deceived as to the essence of what is before you. It's not an actual rose, it's just chemicals. The exact opposite is true with the Eucharist. In fact, the Eucharist is even more "deceiving" in that all of our senses detect only bread and wine. We can break the bread and hear it crack, taste it, etc. Our senses tell us this is bread. But, in essence, it has been transformed into God, in the Person of Jesus the Son.

In order to understand this properly, we need a sort of "sixth sense." We need the spiritual sense of faith. Faith is a gift by which we come to <u>know</u>, with <u>certainty</u>, that this is no longer bread. Rather, it is God. It is the Body, Blood, Soul and Divinity of God the Son.

No amount of study, reasoning, or arguing will convince us of this truth. But faith will. In fact, faith will convince us so deeply that we can come to believe with our whole being. And this is a conviction and level of belief that we can never arrive at using only our five senses or reasoning ability.

If this is hard to believe then it's a sign that God wants to deepen your faith in the Eucharist. He wants you to meet His divine presence there in the depth of your soul. He wants you to know Him, love Him, adore Him and surrender your life to Him in this precious gift.

If you want to fully grasp the Mass, and understand the full meaning of the Holy Eucharist, then you must understand this most precious gift from three perspectives. All three, together, make up the full meaning and reality of the Eucharist. These three perspectives are: Sacrifice, Sacrament, and Communion. Let's start with Sacrifice.

## The One Eternal Sacrifice

We must begin with an understanding of the Sacrifice of Christ on the Cross. Jesus, the Son of God, took on our fallen human nature and died for us once and for all. In His suffering and death He destroyed death itself by rising victorious. But His death was a real death, and it was the perfect sacrifice and atonement for all our sins.

Therefore, the Mass is called, among many things, "The Holy Sacrifice." It is called this because that is what it is. Look at it this way. Jesus' death on the Cross took place almost 2,000 years ago. We were not there. Or were we? The truth is that every time we participate in the Mass we are present at Calvary. And we are not only present, we are participants. Every time we attend the Mass it is as if time ceases and we enter into this timeless moment of the Sacrifice of Christ. We are there, not so much historically; rather, we are there essentially, truly and spiritually. Our soul is present to the

Sacrifice of the Cross and we are able to share in the fruits of that Sacrifice.

Again, this takes faith to understand, believe and experience. But remember that faith is not just believing. Faith is knowing. In this case, it's a "knowing" that enables us to also participate in that which takes place. Faith enables us to share in the one Sacrifice of Christ on the Cross made present to us through the Holy Sacrifice of the Mass.

Perhaps that's a bit deep. The Eucharist is deep! The Sacrifice of the Mass is a profound reality like none other. Sit and prayerfully ponder it. God will help you understand and make sense of it. And when you do begin to understand, you will start to appreciate the Mass like you never have before.

## The Divine Sacrament Made Present

The Last Supper was the beginning act of the Sacrifice of the Cross. At that first Mass, Jesus took bread and said, "Take this, all of you, and eat of it. This is my Body." He then took the precious chalice of wine and said, "This is my Blood."

It's important to see that this Last Supper, the first Mass, continued from that Holy Thursday evening, through Friday on the Cross and culminated in the Resurrection on Sunday. The Mass is this entire event of Jesus' life, death and resurrection all in one.

The fruit of the Mass is the gift of His True Presence under the appearance of bread and wine. This is the Sacrament of His Body and Blood. By "Sacrament" we mean here that the same God in Heaven, the same Eternal Son, is made present to us under the form of bread and wine. So, as we genuflect and kneel before the Holy Eucharist, we are kneeling before God Himself. This is an amazing reality and one that should leave us in awe every time we enter a church and see the tabernacle. It's an amazing reality that should draw us into an adoration chapel where the Eucharist is exposed for us to pray before. God is truly with us in this precious gift.

## Transforming Communion

As we said above, the Sacrifice of the Cross is made present through the celebration of the Mass. The fruit of this Sacrifice is the Sacramental True Presence of Christ our Lord hidden under the form of bread and wine. But these two essential aspects are not the end. God wants to take this wondrous gift one step further. He wants to unite Himself with us through Holy Communion. It is a command of Christ that we attend Mass every Sunday and holy day of obligation, but it's an act of love that invites us to a worthy reception of Holy Communion.

Holy Communion is the ultimate goal of the Eucharist. The reason Christ sacrificed Himself on the Cross and offered Himself in His Body and Blood is so that we can receive Him into our very soul through Holy Communion. This is what it's all about. This is the pinnacle! In fact, the Holy Eucharist is spoken of as both the source of our Christian life and also the summit. What a grace!

"Communion" means "union with." And "union" means there is a transformation of two into one. That, of course, is what the reception of Holy Communion does. It enables us to let Jesus unite Himself with us in our human nature. And in this unity, we share not only in His death, we also share in His resurrection from death. This death to sin and resurrection to new life now become part of who we are. And this is what the Christian life is all about. We see these truths clearly revealed in John's Gospel:

> Jesus said to them, "Amen, amen, I say to you, unless you eat the flesh of the Son of Man and drink his blood, you do not have life within you. Whoever eats my flesh and drinks my blood has eternal life, and I will raise him on the last day. For my flesh is true food, and my blood is true drink. Whoever eats my flesh and drinks my blood remains in me and I in him. (John 6:53-56)

The last line, especially, reveals the unity that is established as a result of reception of the Holy Eucharist. To have Jesus remain in us and we in Him is the ultimate fruit of the Holy Mass.

## The Mass Explained

The Mass follows a set liturgical formula which, in itself, is filled with meaning. The many meanings within this ritual action of the Mass can easily be missed. Let's walk through the entire Mass and briefly touch on its meaning. Understanding what we do, why we do it and what it all means will help us to celebrate the Mass with much deeper faith and devotion.

**Entrance Rite:** This beginning part of the Mass can be broken up into four parts: 1) Procession (with entrance antiphon); 2) Act of Penance; 3) Gloria; 4) Opening Prayer. The ultimate purpose of this entire rite is to ensure that the faithful, who come together as one, establish communion and dispose themselves to listen properly to God's Word and to celebrate the Eucharist worthily. Let's look at each part of this entrance rite and highlight the meaning found within.

*Entrance Antiphon (song):* The purpose of this chant is to begin the celebration of the holy Mass, to foster unity among all those present, to draw their thoughts into the wondrous mystery of the particular liturgical season or celebration, and to accompany the liturgical procession of the priest celebrant and the ministers who will assist with the Mass. This is done through the beautiful act of singing. The many voices join together in the one melodious proclamation of faith. The ideal is that the antiphon of the day is sung. However, it is permissible that another appropriate song be sung. The key here is the unity established by the song and text of that song.

*Procession:* As the song is sung, the procession takes place. It is led by the Cross which symbolizes that our journey through this world toward Heaven is made possible only by the Cross. The Mass servers and the ordained ministers participate in the procession. They, together, represent all the faithful on this journey toward Heaven.

*Greeting:* 1) The Sign of the Cross begins the greeting. This is a powerful gesture. We call on God's Name, Father, Son and Holy Spirit, which should always be the beginning of prayer. 2) The priest then says, "The Lord be with you." This initial greeting is a reassurance of God's love and fidelity to be with each person who approaches the Holy Mass and offers a promise of His presence in their lives so as to fulfill the mission He is giving them as Christians.

3) The congregation then responds, "And with your spirit." This is not simply a friendly gesture as if to say "greetings and blessings to you, too, father!" Rather, the reference to the priest's "spirit" is a reference to his ordination. Thus, it is an acknowledgment on the part of the faithful that the priest is there in the person of Christ by virtue of his ordination. So they are actually acknowledging Christ's presence as the Liturgy begins. This should also remind us that the role of the priest, at that moment, is to be a sacramental minister and instrument of Christ. Therefore, it's not his time to be funny or to emphasize his personality. Rather, the priest must strive to "disappear" so to speak and strive to conform himself to the Person of Christ.

*Act of Penance:* The act of penance is all about preparation. If you had a party at your house you would prepare for it. Or, if you had an important project at work, you'd prepare. So it is with the Mass. The best way we can prepare is to seek the mercy of God through the forgiveness of our sins. Of course, seeking God's mercy and forgiveness is something we must do every day, all day. But, even if we just went to confession prior to Mass, it is appropriate to insert this immediate preparation for Mass in the opening rites.

One option for this act of penance is to pray the *Confiteor* (I confess to almighty God...). In this prayer, we make a triple acknowledgment of our sins by saying, "Through my fault, through my fault, through my most grievous fault." While speaking this, we are to strike our breast as a sign of our sorrow.

We also speak the Greek *Kyrie* at this moment. The Greek ties us to ancient Christians since this was the language they spoke. It is the only Greek we use in the Liturgy in the Latin Rite. We say, *Kyrie eleison, Christe eleison, Kyrie eleison* (Lord have mercy, Christ have mercy, Lord have mercy). Again, we have a triple plea for mercy. Three is the number of perfection and fullness and, therefore, is a way of saying, "Lord, please shower the perfection and fullness of your mercy upon us."

*Gloria:* The *Gloria* is a response to the Kyrie. Just as cooking prepares for a meal or Advent prepares for Christmas, so also begging for mercy prepares us to receive it. Therefore, upon asking for mercy we immediately rejoice with the *Gloria* as a way of acknowledging that the mercy we have asked for is given to us.

*Opening Prayer:* The priest then says or sings, "Let us pray." He takes a moment of silence and then prays the prayer called the "Collect." This prayer gathers all the prayers of the faithful into one and offers them to the Father. This prayer concludes the Introductory Rites.

**Liturgy of the Word**: The Liturgy of the Word includes the following parts of the Mass: 1) First Reading; 2) Psalm; 3) Second Reading (on Sundays and Solemnities only); 4) Gospel; 5) Homily; 6) Creed (on Sundays and Solemnities only); 7) Prayers of the Faithful.

God is truly present in this world in many ways. Scripture is one of those ways that God makes Himself present to us. When the Scriptures are proclaimed, Christ Himself is proclaimed and made present. Therefore, the Liturgy of the Word is a true manifestation of Christ through the hearing of the Word of God.

There is one subtle aspect of the Liturgy of the Word that reveals our understanding of the presence of Christ in the proclamation of the Scriptures. This subtlety is that, after the readings are proclaimed, the lector says, "The Word of the Lord." And after the Gospel is proclaimed, the priest or deacon says, "The Gospel of the Lord." The wording of that conclusion acknowledges that the "Word of God" was just made present, not just the "words of God." In other words, the proclamation of Scripture is a manifestation of Jesus, the Eternal Word. The Scriptures are alive. The Word of God is living. God is truly present as His Word is proclaimed. He is the Word that is proclaimed. The Word is a Person before it is spoken or written.

Contrast this to a public reading of something like the U.S. Constitution. A public reading of this document does not *literally* make the founding fathers present to us; rather, it only makes present their words and ideas. But Scripture is much different. By being a Living Word, we understand that Jesus is very much alive and that the hearing of Scripture is a hearing of the literal Person of Christ Himself. He is there. This reveals that in the Liturgy of the Word, we do not just hear *about* God or His ideas; rather, we hear God, meet God and are transformed by God <u>Himself</u>. This also reveals the deeply personal nature of the public reading of the Word of God.

Therefore, the next time you are at Mass, try to understand that, as the Scriptures are proclaimed, Jesus Himself is there speaking to you.

Let's take a look at the various aspects of the Liturgy of the Word in more detail:

*Sunday Readings:* The Sunday readings are on a three year cycle. This means that over a three year period, we hear the entire Bible. We do not actually cover every single verse of the Bible during these three years, but we do cover much of it.

The First Reading and Gospel are, for the most part, tied together. Often, we will hear in the First Reading an Old Testament verse that prefigures or points to its fulfillment in the Gospel. So, for example, in the First Reading we may read about the manna in the desert from the story of the Israelites wandering the desert for forty years. Then, in the Gospel, we may hear about the new manna, the Eucharist. Most of the time there will be a connection, so it's good to try to listen for that connection so as to understand the unity of the Old Testament with the New Testament.

The Psalm is a song of praise and is often read in an antiphonal way (like the refrain of a song being repeated after each verse).

The Second Reading is from the New Testament and is often an exhortation. It comes from a letter in the New Testament, the Acts of the Apostles, or Revelation. This reading stands on its own and is not intentionally tied to the Gospel or Old Testament except for special feasts.

The Gospel is the culmination of the Liturgy of the Word and stands out for its reverence. We stand, sing the Alleluia, have a procession with the Gospel book and may use incense and candles. It is also read only by the priest or deacon. The Gospel is not only a sharing of the very words and actions of Christ; it is also a proclamation of the very Person of Christ, the Word of God. This proclamation presents us with the fullness of revelation.

*Homily:* The homily is not simply a talk or explanation of the Scriptures. The homily is actually part of the Liturgy itself. Therefore, it is a prayer. And as a prayer, it is a heart to heart conversation between God and His people. Sure, not every homily is experienced that way, but if we are open, we will discover that God will speak to us. This happens all the more when the priest or deacon is truly immersed in Christ by his personal holiness. But it can also happen even when the homilist is not particularly holy. God speaks regardless of the instrument and we ought to listen.

The homily also presumes one listens in faith. In other words, it is not necessarily an initial evangelization or teaching of the faith. It's spoken from the heart of Jesus to the hearts of the faithful, those who already believe. However, even this experience will have the effect of helping to evangelize those who need it the most.

*Creed:* The Creed is the public profession of our faith. It's a tightly packed summary of all that we believe. The Creed is summarized in Book One of this series, *My Catholic Faith!*, so if you have not had the opportunity to read that book, your weekly profession of the Creed at the Sunday Liturgy would be greatly enhanced by doing so.

Remember that "belief," as a response to revelation, produces the gift of faith. This is what should take place in the profession of the Creed. Professing the Creed should not simply be a professing of what we have chosen to believe for other reasons. It must be the fruit of the gift of faith in our souls. It must be the fruit of God speaking to us, revealing Himself to us, and us assenting to that revelation.

Starting in Advent, 2011, the English speaking world began using a new translation of the Mass and, within that new translation, there was a new translation of the Nicene Creed. One notable change to point out is the change from "We believe" to "I believe." This change was made so as to be more faithful to the original Latin text, but it also points to the very personal nature of our profession of faith. Faith must be personal. It must by "my" faith. Strive to make your profession of the faith just that.

*Intercessions:* The Intercessions conclude the Liturgy of the Word and are intended to be "general" intercessions for the entire Church, and by the entire Church. In these General Intercessions, we especially pray for: the Church, the civil authorities, the salvation of the whole world, those burdened by any sort of difficulty (suffering, sick, hurting, evil), local needs, and for those who have died.

So the Liturgy of the Word concludes and gives way to the Liturgy of the Eucharist. The ultimate goal of the Liturgy of the Word is to prepare us to participate more fully in the Liturgy of the Eucharist. It must enkindle within us a deeper faith and a strong desire to move into the celebration of the Sacrifice of Christ on the Cross, the manifestation of His Sacred Body and Blood, and our union with Him in Holy Communion.

**Liturgy of the Eucharist**: The Liturgy of the Eucharist is the highpoint of the Mass. It's also the summit of our entire faith and worship. There is no more perfect way to worship God than to enter into the celebration of the Eucharistic Sacrifice, adore His divine presence and receive Him in Holy Communion.

The Liturgy of the Eucharist involves the following parts: 1) Preparation of the Gifts; 2) Eucharistic Prayer; 3) Communion Rite. Within each of these three parts there are various prayers and gestures of great significance. Let's look at each.

*Preparation of the Gifts:* This part of the Mass includes the preparation of the altar, the presentation of the gifts of bread and wine, and the preparation of those gifts at the altar by the priest and deacon. This action is also called the "offertory" which better illustrates the sacrificial nature of the action.

After the altar is prepared with the chalice, Missal, cloths, etc., there are the basic gifts offered: *bread and wine.* Some cultures also offer: wax (for candles), flowers, fruit, wool (for vestments), honey, oil, and money. Most often only bread and wine are brought forward but any of these gifts may be presented. Additionally, in some cultures there are gifts brought forward for the sustenance of the priest such as fruit, honey and oil. These gifts should come from the hard work of one's hands which represents the personal investment through the sacrifice of labor. The priest acknowledges this fact in the prayer he prays as the gifts are initially offered to God. He says they are "fruit of the earth and work of human hands (a joint gift from God and His people)."

Bread symbolized basic sustenance in the ancient world (not just a side dish), and wine symbolized the gift of superabundance. God does not need our gifts, rather, He invites us to enter into His offering because we need to give. Additionally, in the offering we should see our lives and our personal sacrifices presented to God. As the gift of wine is prepared, the priest states, "by the mystery of this water and wine may we come to share in the divinity of Christ who humbled Himself to share in our humanity." As he says this, he adds a drop of water to the chalice which symbolizes humanity being immersed in divinity. We are that single drop and we must become consumed by the Blood of Christ and His divinity.

The priest then washes his hands, which is symbolic of him purifying himself before entering into the "Holy of Holies." Afterwards, he addresses the congregation with the following: "Pray brethren that <u>my sacrifice and yours</u>..." This is important because it indicates that there are two sacrifices taking place, united as one. First, there is the sacrifice the priest is offering which is the one Sacrifice of Christ. Second, there is the sacrifice the people offer which is their own personal sacrifice united to the Sacrifice of Christ. This unity of sacrifices ensures that the sacrifices we bring will be received by the Father as if they were coming from Christ the Son.

**Eucharistic Prayer:** The Eucharistic Prayer can be broken up into ten different parts. Let's briefly look at each one of these so as to gain a deeper understanding of the meaning and effect of this prayer.

The *Preface* begins with "The Lord be with you." It continues with an exchange of statements of faith and then the priest enters into a prayer of thanksgiving. This prayer concludes by acknowledging that we are joined by the angels and saints in their song of praise.

The song of praise we pray with the angels and saints is the *Sanctus*. *Sanctus* means "holy" and is repeated three times to state that God is thrice holy, or, the holiest of all. We cry out, "Holy, holy, holy..." This also shows we are joined with the Heavenly Liturgy as seen in the Book of Revelation 4:8.

*Epiclesis*: The third Eucharistic Prayer uses the following words for the epiclesis: "Make holy, therefore, these gifts, we pray, by sending down your spirit upon them like the dewfall." This prayer is the calling down of the Holy Spirit upon the gifts so as to begin their transformation from ordinary bread and wine into the Body and Blood of Christ.

*Words of Consecration*: The priest then enters into the heart and center of the Eucharistic Prayer by repeating the very words of Jesus as He instituted the Eucharist at the Last Supper. He says, "This is my Body...this is my Blood." With the proclamation of these words, the bread and wine are transformed into the Body, Blood, Soul and Divinity of Christ Jesus.

*Mysterium Fidei*: The priest states, "The Mystery of Faith." This acknowledges the sacramental presence of Christ on the altar, the fruit of the Consecration. It's a statement of faith and the people respond with an acclamation of faith, expressing profound wonder and awe at the incredible mystery before us such as "Save us Savior of the world, for by Your Cross and Resurrection, You have set us free."

*Anamnesis*: In this prayer the priest expresses our need to tell God what we participate in – the offering of His Son to Him! For example, "Therefore, O Lord, we celebrate the memorial of the saving Passion of Your Son, his wondrous Resurrection and Ascension into Heaven..." In this prayer we recall that we now celebrate the memorial of His suffering and death so as to share in the Resurrection. We also thank Him for the joy of being able to participate in this precious gift.

*Offering*: The priest now offers himself and the Church, uniting us all to the one Sacrifice of Christ offered to the Father. Once united to the Sacrifice of Christ, we offer ourselves to the Father in Christ as He is offered to the Father.

*Intercessions*: The priest then prays for those present at the Mass, for all who are in a state of grace (the whole Church), and for all who have died and are receiving the grace from this Mass.

*Doxology*: "Through Him, with Him and in Him..." This prayer, prayed by the priest as he lifts the Body and Blood of Christ, echoes the words of St. Paul in that all things are done in, with and through God for His glory (see Ephesians 1). The doxology is then affirmed by God's people with the great Amen!

**The Rite of Holy Communion**: The Rite of Holy Communion encompasses all the prayers and actions that immediately prepare us to receive this precious gift. These include: 1) The Our Father; 2) The Sign of Peace; 3) The Fractioning; 4) The "Beholding;" 5) Holy Communion; 6) The Communion antiphon; 7) The Closing Prayer; 8) The Blessing. Let's look at each of these actions in more detail.

*Our Father:* This prayer will be covered in more detail in Chapter Eleven, but we should also say a few words about it here. The "Our Father" prayer establishes the fact that, because of our "Communion" with Jesus, we are also children of the Father. We are brothers and sisters of Christ and, therefore, also children of His Father. This prayer also reveals and professes our continual entering into a deeper intimacy with the Father through Communion with Jesus.

*Sign of peace:* Communion not only establishes a deeper unity with God, it also establishes a deeper unity and intimacy with one another. Thus, the Sign of Peace is a symbolic way of expressing the communion we have with one another.

*Fractioning:* In the fractioning the priest breaks the Host in two and then drops a small piece in the chalice full of the Precious Blood. There are two meanings here to point out. 1) This reveals a connection with the pope. There was an early custom of bringing a fragment from the pope's Mass to other churches and placing that fragment in the chalices at each church as a way of showing the unity between all of the faithful united under the Holy Father. 2) During the Eucharistic Prayer there is a separate consecration of the Body and Blood. The fact that they are consecrated separately points to the death of Christ (the separation of Christ's Body and Blood by the pouring out of His blood). But during this rite there is a commingling of the two. This commingling points to the Resurrection in that the Body and Blood now are joined together once again.

*The "Beholding:"* Next, the priest holds up the host and proclaims, "Behold the Lamb of God, behold Him who takes away the sins of the world. Blessed are those called to the supper of the Lamb." These are the words of St. John the Baptist as Jesus came walking toward him to be baptized (see John 1:29). They reveal the sacrificial aspect of the Mass by calling Jesus the "Lamb of God." He was the Lamb who was the Sacrifice for our sins.

In response to beholding the Lamb, we say, "Lord, I am not worthy that you should enter under my roof, but only say the word and my soul shall be healed." This is an expression of humility and faith and is taken from the words of the Roman centurion when he did not feel worthy to have Jesus come to his house to heal his servant (see Matthew 8:8).

*Holy Communion*: Now we come to the ultimate reason Jesus offered the Sacrifice of His life and memorialized it in the Mass; namely, so that we could receive Him in Holy Communion. St. Thérèse of Lisieux reveals the proper disposition we should have for Holy Communion in her autobiography, "Story of a Soul." She says about her first Holy Communion:

> How lovely it was, that first kiss of Jesus in my heart – it was truly a kiss of love. I knew that I was loved and said, "I love You, and I give myself to You forever." Jesus asked for nothing, He claimed no sacrifice. Long before that, He and little Thérèse had seen and understood one another well, but on that day it was more than a meeting – it was a complete fusion. We were no longer two, for Thérèse had disappeared like a drop of water lost in the mighty ocean. Jesus alone remained – the Master and the King.

Holy Communion must become deeply personal and deeply intimate. It must become that divine "fusion" St. Thérèse spoke of. In the reception of this holy Sacrament our hearts and souls are made one with Christ, if we let Him in. And that's the key. We have to let Him in.

Receiving Holy Communion is not automatic. Just because we walk up in the communion line and receive Him doesn't mean that we have truly <u>received Him</u>. We have to dispose ourselves, prepare ourselves and let Him come to us and draw us into the communion He desires with us. Our responsibility is to respond openly and generously to His invitation to divine union.

*Communion Antiphon:* The Communion Antiphon, which can also be a hymn, has the effect of uniting all those receiving Communion. It also provides meditation on the theme of the Mass, Scripture of the day, or liturgical season.

*Closing Prayer:* The Closing Prayer concludes the Rite of Communion by acknowledging what we have just received in a prayer of thanks and petition that our Communion will bear much fruit.

*Blessing:* The priest concludes the Mass by the blessing in the Name of the Father, and of the Son and of the Holy Spirit and the deacon then proclaims the dismissal. Two of the options for the dismissal are, "Go and announce the Gospel of the Lord" and, "Go in peace, glorifying the Lord by your life." These words of dismissal present a clear commission to bring Christ to the world. Our communion with God must have the effect of overflowing into our daily life. We must evangelize to the ends of the Earth!

Hopefully this summary of the various parts of the Holy Mass will help you enter more deeply into worship in a personal and committed way each time you attend. The Mass is the greatest act on Earth and we should be in awe every time we attend!

# 6

# THE SACRAMENT OF PENANCE

"Those who approach the Sacrament of Penance obtain pardon from God's mercy for the offense committed against him, and are, at the same time, reconciled with the Church which they have wounded by their sins and which by charity, by example, and by prayer labors for their conversion" (LG 11 § 2) (*CCC* #1422)

The Sacrament of Penance is given many names. The various names highlight its effects in our lives. Here are the various names we use:

**Sacrament of Penance**: This sacrament allows us to do acts of penance for our sins as a way of deepening our conversion and turning away from the sins we confess.

**Sacrament of Conversion**: It calls us to change, to convert and to become more conformed to the image of Christ.

**Sacrament of Confession**: In this sacrament we are called to disclose our conscience and reveal our sins in absolute confidentiality to the priest.

**Sacrament of Forgiveness**: The ultimate effect of this sacrament is forgiveness of our sins.

**Sacrament of Reconciliation**: By receiving this sacrament we are not only reconciled to God, we are also reconciled to the other members of the Church.

When a person is baptized, every sin is forgiven. Of course, if we were baptized as infants, there were no "personal" sins present, only "original sin." In that case, original sin is wiped away. But for those who are baptized as adults, they should be pleased to know that every sin of their past is fully wiped away at baptism. As mentioned in Chapter Three, in the early Church there were those who actually waited to be baptized until later in life so that they could receive this effect of Baptism closer to death. But if we have a proper understanding of both Baptism and Penance, we will realize that infant baptism is the ideal when followed by regular participation in the Sacrament of Penance. St. Ambrose is quoted in the *Catechism* to illustrate this by saying, "there are water and tears: the water of Baptism and the tears of repentance" (St. Ambrose, ep. 41, 12: PL 16, 1116). (*CCC #1429*)

The key to understanding the Sacrament of Penance is to understand how glorious it is to embrace a life of ongoing conversion. This is the Christian life! It's a life of continually growing closer to God and moving further away from our sins. For some, this can seem like a burden and can be undesirable. But if we understood the wonderful interior rewards of ongoing and deepening conversion, it would be our greatest desire.

How do we convert? First and foremost, it's an interior action. It means we discover two things in the depths of our conscience. We discover sin, and we discover God. The goal is obviously to see sin for what it is, and then to turn it over to our merciful God. But God also wants this interior conversion to have exterior aspects. Hence, we have the Sacrament of Penance. In this sacrament we invite Christ, in the person of the priest, to enter into our conscience and to wipe it clean leaving only God there to consume us more fully.

This interior conversion also has the exterior effect of changing our actions and enabling God to shine through us in a more manifest way so as to offer His love and mercy to others. So conversion is something first interior which unfolds in our exterior lives.

Let's now take a look at the necessary preparations we must make for the Sacrament of Penance from a more practical point of view. If we can understand this sacrament for what it is, we may also come to accept the value of regularly practicing it!

## How I Prepare

Preparation for the Sacrament of Penance is an ongoing process. It requires a daily acknowledgement of two things. First, we must see God's mercy for what it is. Second, when and only when we understand and believe in God's mercy will we then be properly prepared to fully embrace this sacrament.

Mercy is love. It's the form of love given to us by God. And in order to receive mercy we must understand it. And in order to properly understand mercy, we must understand who God is.

Is God a God of wrath and anger? Is He a God of judgment and justice? Well, yes, He is. But His wrath and anger are holy and are directed at our sins, not us. God hates our sin, but loves us with an infinite love. In fact, the reason He hates our sin so much is because He loves us so much. He knows that our sin hurts us and hinders our ability to love Him and find the fulfillment in life we so deeply seek. God wants us happy and, for that reason, wants us free from sin.

Start with an understanding of an all-powerful God filled with a holy wrath toward that which hurts us most...our sin. Ideally, you will let your own heart grow in the same holy wrath toward your sin. You will ideally let your heart see sin for what it is and grow in a desire to be freed of it so that you can be free to love and live as you were made to live.

God is also a God of judgment and justice. Again, this is good! Why? Because His judgment is perfectly just. It is not harsh or arbitrary. It is not condemning or oppressive. His judgment is grounded only in Truth. And it is that Truth that sets us free.

For this reason, we should desire judgment and justice in our lives. Unfortunately, when we hear the word "judgment" we can think of being "judgmental." God is not judgmental in the way we normally use that word. He does not hold onto our sin and keep it always before us as if to continually say, "You are a sinner, shame on you." No, God's judgment is such that it clears up confusion helping us to sort through that which burdens us the most. So do not be afraid of this pure and holy form of judgment and justice that comes from our loving and merciful God.

Once we have a proper understanding of holy wrath, anger, judgment and justice, we will be in a position to let those holy qualities fill our own souls. We will take on these attributes from God and use them for our own holiness. We will begin to see sin for what it is and deeply desire to be freed of it. What a grace this is!

These good and holy qualities will lead us to practice penance and repentance. Regarding the practice of penance and repentance, the *Catechism* states:

> The interior penance of the Christian can be expressed in many and various ways. Scripture and the Fathers insist above all on three forms, *fasting, prayer,* and *almsgiving* (Tob 12:8; Mt 6:1-18), which express conversion in relation to oneself, to God, and to others. Alongside the radical purification brought about by Baptism or martyrdom they cite as means of obtaining forgiveness of sins: efforts at reconciliation with one's neighbor, tears of repentance, concern for the salvation of one's neighbor, the intercession of the saints, and the practice of charity "which covers a multitude of sins" (1 Pet 4:8; cf. Jas 5:20). (#1434)

**Effort at reconciliation with one's neighbor:** How hard this is! When we have been hurt by another it takes a tremendous amount of mercy to reconcile and forgive. One way to do this is to see the justice of God at work. In God's justice, He desires that all people be saved. The first step in this process is to forgive and offer mercy. This mercy is a form of justice in that it brings about reconciliation. Think about those you need to forgive and be reconciled with. How are you doing at that? If you find yourself lacking, this is a good area to look at and grow in.

**Tears of repentance:** This is simply a holy hatred for our sin that affects even our emotions and passions. It means we are so repulsed by sin that we are consumed with a holy desire to overcome even the smallest weaknesses. Emotions should not be the driving force or else they may cause more problems than they solve. But they play a role when they are directed by the Holy Spirit. Surrender your emotions to God and ask that He fill them with the same passion for freedom that rules His heart, and the same hatred for sin that He has.

**Concern for the salvation of one's neighbor and the practice of charity:** True repentance always looks to the other. We will not sit there self-consumed; rather, we will desire to overcome our sin because it will have a glorious effect in the lives of others. Repentance of our own sin is ultimately done out of charity in that we seek freedom so that we can be a better instrument of grace for them.

**Intercession of the saints:** We are not alone. It's easy to forget that the saints are there praying for us constantly. Remember that! Call on them and rely on them. Let their powerful intercession become an effective means of grace in your life and in the lives of those you are called to love.

The above practices are accomplished when we embrace basic spiritual principles of repentance, penance and ongoing conversion. We must daily read the Scriptures, be faithful to Mass, spend time every day in prayer, practice charitable works and make daily sacrifices (even if it's not Lent!). All of these tried and true spiritual practices will have the effect of preparing us to be freed of our sin. Once prepared, we are ready to enter into the glorious Sacrament of Forgiveness.

## Understanding this Glorious Gift

> Sin is before all else an offense against God, a rupture of communion with him. At the same time it damages communion with the Church. For this reason conversion entails both God's forgiveness and reconciliation with the Church, which are expressed and accomplished liturgically by the Sacrament of Penance and Reconciliation (LG 11). (*Catechism* #1440)

God alone is the one who can forgive sins. But He can do this any way He chooses. And the primary way He has chosen to offer the grace of forgiveness is through the Church. He is the source, but the Church is intimately involved. And among the greatest ways the Church is involved is the Sacrament of Reconciliation. Let's look at some of the practical aspects of this sacrament and its effects so that we will grow in our love for this glorious gift.

**The Ministry of the Church:** The Church is intimately involved in the Sacrament of Reconciliation in two specific ways. First, it is through the ministry of priests that God directly enters in and wipes sin away. This power to forgive was given to the Apostles and handed down through the ages to all those who share in the ordained ministry. The priest forgives but, in reality, it is Christ, in the person of the priest, who forgives. God is the source of all forgiveness and mercy.

We see this power given to the Apostles when, after His Resurrection, Jesus appeared to them, ordained them, and commanded them to forgive. This is in John 20:21-23:

> [Jesus] said to them again, "Peace be with you. As the Father has sent me, so I send you." And when he had said this, he breathed on them and said to them, "Receive the holy Spirit. Whose sins you forgive are forgiven them, and whose sins you retain are retained."

When we sin, we hurt our relationship with God, but we also hurt our relationship with one another and with the entire Church. Therefore, the Sacrament of Reconciliation also reconciles us to the other members of Christ's Body, the Church.

**Forgiveness of Mortal Sin:** Mortal sin is ugly. More will be said on it in Book Three of this series. But for now, suffice it to say that a mortal sin contains three basic elements: 1) It is a grave action against God; 2) We know it is gravely wrong; 3) We fully intend and consent to do it anyway. When all three of these elements are present, we have committed a mortal sin.

By "mortal" we mean that the sin is so serious that it completely severs our relationship with God and His Church. And if we were to die without repenting of this sin, we'd go to Hell. So, yes, that's what makes it so ugly. Mortal sin introduces grave disorder into our lives and affects us in every way: emotionally, spiritually, intellectually, and it weakens our will. The way to freedom and forgiveness is the Sacrament of Confession. In this sacrament, God lifts the heavy burden of mortal sin and restores us to His grace. A good understanding of mortal sin, what it is, and what it is not, is very important in making a good and balanced confession.

We say that Confession is the "ordinary way" to receive forgiveness of mortal sins. This means that the Church does not know of any other way that God forgives. Now we do not want to limit God's mercy and say that it's impossible to receive forgiveness from Him through some other means, but it is important to make clear that this is the only way we <u>know</u> of that God has forgiven us. So if you've struggled with mortal sin, make sure to read on and to embrace this sacrament!

**Forgiveness of Venial Sin:** Very often, sin does not rise to the level of being mortal. Even if the action itself is grave, there are often some diminishing circumstances involved. For example, say someone struggles with some form of sexual addiction such as pornography. This is becoming a very common struggle in our day and age. Looking at pornography is a serious offence against God and so it should be considered grave. However, what about the person who has struggled with this for years and is finally getting help. He is going to confession every week and seeking good spiritual advice as well as the grace of the Sacrament. He has put filters on his computer and has friends keeping him accountable. In other words, he is trying hard to overcome this addiction.

Say this person has done well for weeks and then, in a moment of weakness, falls and looks at some images online. Say he had been very stressed out that week and was momentarily overwhelmed. He feels horrible about it and is repulsed by this fall. Has he just committed a mortal sin? In other words, has he just completely cut off his relationship with God? Perhaps, but probably not. In this case, we do not want to give the impression that he did nothing wrong, because he did. This was certainly sin. But the facts are that his ongoing struggle, his addiction, his honest attempts to overcome this, and his immediate sorrow indicate that this grave action was a venial sin rather than a mortal one. If anything diminishes personal guilt for a serious action, the sin moves into the category of venial rather than mortal. Our moral tradition has recognized that factors such as *force, fear, passion and ignorance* diminish a person's culpability before God.

The point here is definitely NOT to give the impression that it was no big deal. Rather, we need to make sure that we do not overreact to our weakness, temptations and sin. We should be merciful to ourselves in the same way that God is merciful. In this case, the person should immediately say an act of contrition, express sorrow and recommit himself to overcoming this struggle. And he should mention it in his next confession. But he should also be careful not to fall into the trap of thinking that he is now doomed to Hell until his next confession. God does not work that way.

Venial sin is also every other sin that would not fall into the category of "grave" but is still wrong. This would be any of the commandments or capital sins outlined below that are committed to a lesser degree. Venial sin is always with us and it requires a daily commitment to battle against it. Receiving the Eucharist, signing ourselves with holy water, or making a sincere act of contrition will bring God's forgiveness for venial sins. However, what is even more powerful in our battle against every venial sin is taking them to confession. By confessing these sins we allow God to pour forth His healing salve upon the areas we struggle with the most. We let Him strengthen us in our times of need and completely blot out all sin.

The least serious form of venial sin (that which is the least sinful) can be called "spiritual imperfections." These sins manifest the many ways we lack perfect virtue. We are all guilty of these spiritual imperfections and, therefore, always have something to say in confession. Specifically, we are guilty of not having perfect faith, hope and charity. The Sacrament of Confession also helps us in these areas in that the sacramental grace given strengthens us in these virtues to make us more like Christ.

**Seal of Confession:** One of the greatest gifts we receive from the Church is the promise of absolute confidentiality when confessing our sins. The priest can never, under any circumstance, reveal our sins to another. That means, for example, if he is called into civil court and told that he must reveal your confession to the judge and jury, the priest must decline and refuse regardless of the civil consequences against him. He cannot reveal your confession to another priest, to his bishop or to anyone. The seal is absolute! In fact, if a priest were to ever intentionally reveal someone's confession he would automatically and immediately be excommunicated from the Church. Ouch! We take the seal of Confession very seriously!

## From Interior Repentance to the Grace of the Sacrament

Let's look more practically at how this sacrament is celebrated. It follows a certain process and liturgical rite. Within that liturgical celebration the interior intention and action is of utmost importance. Here are the keys you need to know and embrace for a good celebration of this sacrament.

**Examining our Conscience:** We will greatly benefit from examining our Conscience so as to practically see what sin we need to be freed of. There are many forms of examination of conscience but the best ones are based on the Ten Commandments or the Seven Capital Sins. Below are a couple of an examinations that will shed light on what we need to let go of if we want to enter more fully into God's abundant mercy.

### Individual Examination of Conscience – 7 Deadly Sins

**Pride:** "Pride is an untrue opinion of ourselves, an untrue idea of what we are not." Have I a superior attitude in thinking, or speaking or acting? Am I snobbish? Have I offensive, haughty ways of acting or carrying myself? Do I hold myself above others? Do I demand recognition? Do I desire to be always first? Do I seek advice? Am I ready to accept advice? Am I in any sense a "bully"? Am I inclined to be "bossy"? Do I speak ill of others? Have I lied about others? Do I make known the faults of others? Do I seek to place the blame on others, excusing myself? Is there anyone to whom I refuse to speak? Is there anyone to whom I have not spoken for a long time? Am I prone to argue? Am I offensive in my arguments? Have I a superior "know-it-all attitude" in arguments? Am I self-conscious? Am I sensitive? Am I easily wounded?

**Envy:** "Envy is a sadness which we feel, on account of the good that happens to our neighbor." Do I feel sad at the prosperity of others? At their success in games? In athletics? Do I rejoice at their failures? Do I envy the riches of others?

**Sloth:** "Sloth is a kind of cowardice and disgust, which makes us neglect and omit our duties, rather than to discipline ourselves." Have I an inordinate love of rest, neglecting my duties? Do I act lazily? Am I too fond of rest? Do I take lazy positions in answering prayers? Do I kneel in a lounging way? Do I delight in idle conversation? Do I fail to be fervent in the service of God?

**Lust**: "Lust is the love of the pleasures that are contrary to purity." Have I desired or done impure things? Have I taken pleasure in entertaining impure thoughts or desires? Have I read impure material, listened to music with impure lyrics, or looked at impure images, whether in photos or on television or in movies or on the Internet? Have I aroused sexual desire in myself or another by impure kissing, embracing, or touching? Have I committed impure actions alone, i.e., masturbation? Do I dress immodestly or am I too concerned with the way I look? Do I use vulgar language or tell or listen to impure jokes or stories? Have I given into desires of adultery even in my imagination?

**Covetousness:** "Covetousness is a disordered love of the goods of this world." Do I dispose of my money properly or selfishly? Do I discharge my duties in justice to my fellow man? Do I discharge my duties in justice to the Church?

**Gluttony**: "Gluttony is a disordered love of eating and drinking." Do I eat to live or live to eat? Do I drink to excess? Do I get drunk? Do I misuse prescription drugs? Do I use illegal drugs? Have I allowed myself to become addicted to alcohol and/or drugs?

**Anger:** "An emotion of the soul, which leads us violently to repel whatever hurts or displeases us." Am I prone to anger? Does practically any little thing arouse my temper? Am I what is generally termed "a sore-head"? Do I fail to repress the first signs of anger? Do I fail to get along well with everybody? Do I ponder over slights or injuries and even presume them? Do I rejoice at the misfortunes of others? Do I think of means of revenge? Of "getting even"? Am I of an argumentative disposition? Have I a spirit of contradiction? Am I given to ridicule of persons, places, or things? Am I hard to get along with? Do I carry grudges, remain "on the outs" with anyone? Do I talk about the faults of others? Do I reveal the faults or defects of others? Do I reveal the faults of others from the wrong motive?

## Individual Examination of Conscience – 10 Commandments

**First Commandment: "I am the Lord your God, you shall not have strange gods before Me."** Have I denied God? Have I been ashamed of or denied my faith in front of others? Have I ridiculed the teachings or practices of the Church? Have I neglected my prayers? Have I used witchcraft, Wicca, or other Occult practices? Have I practiced various forms of superstition such as fortune tellers, mediums, ouija boards, tarot cards?

**Second Commandment: "Do not take the name of the Lord in vain."** Do I use God's name carelessly, in anger, or in surprise? Have I called down evil upon anyone or anything?

**Third Commandment: "Keep holy the Sabbath Day."** Have I, through my own fault, failed to come to Mass each Sunday and every Holy Day of Obligation? Do I arrive at Mass late or leave early without good reason? Do I allow myself to be distracted at Mass?

**Fourth Commandment: "Honor your father and mother."** Have I disobeyed my parents or treated them with disrespect? Am I disrespectful, impolite, or discourteous toward my family? Have I neglected my work or my studies? Have I been helpful in my home? Have I failed to study seriously and with diligence? Have I missed an exam at school because of laziness? Am I disrespectful toward the elderly? Am I disobedient to the civil law or to those in authority such as the police?

**Fifth Commandment: "You shall not kill."** Did I have an abortion or help another to have an abortion? Have I mutilated my body or another's body? Did I attempt suicide or seriously consider thoughts of suicide? Do I act violently by fighting or hitting others? Have I had thoughts of hatred toward another? Have I taken illegal drugs or abused prescription drugs? Have I sold or distributed illegal drugs? Do I neglect to take proper care of my body? Do I eat too much, or sleep too much? Do I drink beer or other alcoholic beverages in excess? Have I allowed myself to become intoxicated? Am I too concerned about my health or appearance? Do I deliberately harbor unkind and revengeful thoughts about others? Have I taken revenge? Have I used harsh or abusive language toward another? Do I act rudely, impolitely, or ridicule others? Have I been guilty of the sin of racism? Am I cruel to animals?

**Sixth & Ninth Commandments: "Do not commit adultery. Do not covet your neighbors wife."** Have I desired or done impure things? Have I taken pleasure in entertaining impure thoughts or desires? Have I read impure material, listened to music with impure lyrics, or looked at impure images, whether in photos or on television or in movies or on the Internet? Have I aroused sexual desire in myself or another by impure kissing, embracing, or touching? Have I committed impure actions alone, i.e., masturbation? Have I committed homosexual acts or other unnatural acts? Do I use artificial contraception whether surgical, barrier or chemical methods? Have I dressed immodestly or been too concerned with the way I look? Do I use vulgar language or tell or listen to impure jokes or stories?

**Seventh and tenth Commandments: "You shall not steal. Do not covet your neighbor's goods."** Have I taken anything that was not my own? Have I damaged private or public property or defaced it by vandalism? Have I been guilty of shop-lifting? Have I accepted or bought stolen property or helped someone to steal? Have I bribed someone? Do I gamble excessively? Have I borrowed something without the owner's permission? Have I failed to return something I borrowed? Do I waste money or spend it extravagantly? Have I harbored a greed for money or worldly possessions? Have I made of money, or any possession, a false god? Do I waste goods or food? Have I cheated on tests or schoolwork? Have I cheated in games or sports?

**Eighth Commandment: "You shall not bear false witness against your neighbor."** Have I lied deliberately? Have I sworn to do something sinful or illegal? Have I slandered others by attributing to them sins they did not commit or of which I had no evidence? Do I gossip about others or listen to gossip? Have I told a secret I was asked to keep? Have I betrayed someone's trust? Have I criticized anyone uncharitably? Do I make rash judgments and harbor false suspicions about others? Have I deliberately misled or deceived anyone? Have I refused to forgive someone or held a grudge against him or her? Have I failed to apologize or make amends to someone I offended?

**Other considerations:** Am I greedy or selfish or do I indulge in self-pity? Am I proud or vain or do I show off? Am I superficial and worldly? Do I desire to be praised by exaggerating my success? Am I touchy and hypersensitive? Do I magnify the least oversight or thoughtlessness into an insult or deliberate slight? Have I been boastful? Have I been arrogant with others? Have I obstinately defended actions which are sinful, either my own or other's? Am I rebellious? Have I spent useless time planted before the TV when I could be doing more constructive things? Am I envious of someone's possessions and do I inordinately desire them to be my own? Do I take delight in the misfortunes of others?

OK, so you've let God reveal to you your sin and you now desire to overcome it. What's next? After spending sufficient time with an examination of conscience, it's key to let that examination foster true contrition. Contrition for sin is one of the most important parts of this sacrament, and it all depends on us!

**Contrition:** Contrition has been spoken of in two basic ways: 1) Imperfect contrition; 2) Perfect contrition. Obviously, the latter is what we should aim for.

Imperfect contrition is a sorrow for our sins because we fear punishment. By analogy, it would be like a child who is tempted to take a cookie but refrains because he knows his mom will find out and he will get punished. It is the fear of punishment that keeps him from disobedience. Or, an even clearer example may be if that same child hits his brother and gets in trouble for it. He is told, "If you do not say you are sorry you will have to go to your room!" The boy reluctantly says, "I'm sorry." He is sorry due to fear of punishment.

In our spiritual lives the same is true. We often fear punishment, and more specifically, we may fear Hell. This holy fear of going to Hell is a good starting point in fostering a contrite (sorrowful) heart. Though this is not the ideal and perfect form of sorrow, God accepts it and works with it. Therefore, if we were to go to the Sacrament of Reconciliation and confess a serious sin with imperfect contrition, God would accept our contrition. In this case, the confession may look like this: "Father, forgive me for (mentions serious sin)… I do not want to go to Hell so I ask you to please forgive me." OK, God will forgive you. It is sufficient.

Sufficient, yes, but far from ideal! What is the ideal? The ideal is "perfect contrition." Perfect contrition is a sorrow that says, "I'm sorry for what I did because I love you and I see that my sin hurt that love. I want to repair what I've done and, so, I'm sorry because I do love you."

Perfect contrition is based in love and is motivated by love. It's not motivated by a selfish fear but it is motivated by a different form of "fear." It's the Gift of fear given as one of the Seven Gifts of the Holy Spirit: The gift of "Fear of the Lord." This is a "fear" based love of God or another in that we love the other so much we fear doing anything that hurts them and our relationship with them.

Similarly, let's say spouses love each other so deeply that they are always in tune with what will help or hurt their relationship. The holy fear they experience is not motivated by avoiding conflict, rather, this form of holy fear is that they want their love to keep deepening and want to make sure nothing gets in the way. This holy fear is a driving force to always keep them recommitting themselves to their relationship.

So it is with our relationship with God, having perfect contrition for our sins means we love God so deeply that this love, and the possibility of losing or harming this love, becomes the motivating factor for our contrition. This is the kind of contrition we should strive for in confession.

In the section later in this chapter on how to go to Confession, there is a traditional Act of Contrition. This is a beautiful prayer that clearly expresses both forms of contrition. It states that we are sorry because of God's "just punishments." But it goes on to say, "most of all because they have offended You, my God, who are all-good and deserving of all my love."

**Firm Purpose of Amendment:** The Act of Contrition concludes with a firm purpose of amendment by saying, "I firmly resolve, with the help of Your grace, to sin no more and to avoid the near occasion of sin." This is hard to mean and harder to do. It expresses that we are not only deeply sorry, but we are also committed to change. This firm purpose of amendment is very important if we wish to let the grace of this sacrament transform us.

**Celebrating the Sacrament:** The actual form of the Sacrament of Penance, meaning the practical way we celebrate it, has taken on various forms over the ages. In the early Church it was offered to serious sinners once in their lifetimes. The public sinner would have to do public penance, sometimes for years, before he was given the grace of the Sacrament of Reconciliation. However, in the seventh century the Irish missionaries began the practice of offering this sacrament in a private way. Penance and the confession of sin no longer involved the entire Church. This opened the door for a more frequent celebration of Reconciliation which evolved into the practice we have today where this sacrament is encouraged to be a regular part of our spiritual lives. Some suggest it be celebrated weekly, others suggest monthly and others suggest it be celebrated at least once or twice a year in Advent and Lent. Perhaps a good goal would be to practice it monthly or bi-monthly unless you feel the need to go more often. The Church only *requires* that we go once a year when we are aware of serious sin, but this is a bottom line requirement. We should aim much higher!

The form of this sacrament today is quite simple. The priest guides you through it if you are not well versed in how to do it. Here is the most common way to celebrate this sacrament:

## How to Go to Confession

Begin by saying: ***In the Name of the Father, and of the Son, and of the Holy Spirit. Amen.***

***Bless me, father, for I have sinned. It has been*** (how long?) ***since my last confession and these are my sins…***

**(confess all your sins…be not afraid!).**

After you confess your sins, the priest gives you a penance and then ask you to pray an Act of Contrition:

## ACT OF CONTRITION

**O my God, I am heartily sorry for having offended You, and I detest all my sins because of Your just punishments,**

**but most of all of because they offend You, my God, who are all-good and deserving of all my love. I firmly resolve, with the help of Your grace, to sin no more and to avoid the near occasion of sin. Amen.**

The priest then prays the prayer of absolution (forgiveness).

If your penance is to say some prayers, immediately go say those prayers, or do whatever penance is given.

**You are forgiven!**

**Absolution:** Among the many things we say about this Sacrament of Reconciliation, the central teaching we should cling to with much gratitude is the gift of absolution. Absolution means that once we have done our part by preparing, cultivating contrition, and confessing, God then does His part. He absolves all sin. This is done through the ministry of the priest and is imparted to us through the prayer of absolution. Once the priest prays it over us, our sins are wiped clean!

**Satisfaction and Penance:** We cannot ever make up for our sins, but we must, nonetheless, strive to do penance for them. The *Catechism* states it this way:

> Many sins wrong our neighbor. One must do what is possible in order to repair the harm (e.g., return stolen goods, restore the reputation of someone slandered, pay compensation for injuries). Simple justice requires as much. But sin also injures and weakens the sinner himself, as well as his relationships with God and neighbor. Absolution takes away sin, but it does not remedy all the disorders sin has caused (Council of Trent (1551): DS 1712). Raised up from sin, the sinner must still recover his full spiritual health by doing something more to make amends for the sin: he must "make satisfaction for" or "expiate" his sins. This satisfaction is also called "penance." (#1459)

This happens by the priest assigning you a certain penance. The penance, according to the *Catechism*, could be any of the following: "prayer, an offering, works of mercy, service of neighbor, voluntary self-denial, sacrifices, and above all the patient acceptance of the cross we must bear" (#1460). Hopefully the priest will examine your situation and give some good spiritual advice and assign a penance that will help you toward conversion and freedom from sin. But it's not magic! It's up to you to let the grace enter into your heart and soul and, from there, transform your actions.

Receiving forgiveness is primarily up to God. Working to be completely purified of our sin and the effects of our sin is the next big commitment we must make. In addition to the penance the priest gives us in Confession, we must strive to do additional penances. One grace that goes hand-in-hand with receiving the Sacrament of Penance is the act of receiving an indulgence. Let's now look at how this gift provides the grace needed to overcome our attachment to the sins we have confessed.

## Forgiveness is Not Enough...The Grace of Indulgences

This seems like a strange subheading for this chapter, but it's true. Forgiveness is not enough to grow holy. Here is a classic question that illustrates the point.

Often it is asked whether someone will go straight to Heaven if they go to confession, confess all their sins, and as they walk out of the church have a heart attack and die. They were just forgiven so this must mean they go straight to Heaven with no time in Purgatory! Right? Wrong.

The Sacrament of Reconciliation does in fact forgive all our sins. For that reason, someone who goes to confession and dies prior to committing an unrepented mortal sin will, indeed, go to Heaven. But getting into Heaven also requires something else. It requires complete freedom from all attachment to sin! And that's a tall order.

Sin not only hurts our relationship with God, it also strengthens our "relationship" so to speak with sin itself. In other words, the more we sin, the more we are attached to sin. Confession forgives our past sins, and helps us overcome future sins, but we do need additional grace to be freed from the "attachment" we experience.

For example, say someone is a habitual liar. They have become so used to lying that they do it for no real reason. The habit is deep and strong and they practice it daily and throughout the day.

Now let's say that person goes to confession and receives forgiveness for all past sins of lying. That's excellent! But does this mean that as soon as the person walks out of the confessional they have also completely broken the habit they have formed? Certainly not. Most likely, within a few hours, they will be tempted to lie again simply because the habit is strong within them. This fact reveals to us that forgiveness is not enough, we also need a special grace to help us become detached from all tendencies toward sin. And this is where an indulgence comes in.

The *Catechism* defines an indulgence in the following way:

> "An indulgence is a remission before God of the temporal punishment due to sins whose guilt has already been forgiven, which the faithful Christian who is duly disposed gains under certain prescribed conditions through the action of the Church which, as the minister of redemption, dispenses and applies with authority the treasury of the satisfactions of Christ and the saints" (Paul VI, apostolic constitution, Indulgentiarum doctrina, Norm 1). "An indulgence is partial or plenary according as it removes either part or all of the temporal punishment due to sin" (Indulgentiarum doctrina, Norm 2; cf. Norm 3). The faithful can gain indulgences for themselves or apply them to the dead (CIC, can. 994). (#1471)

Now there is a lot packed into this statement which may be confusing. So let's look at it one piece at a time.

**Temporal Punishment:** First of all, punishment due to sin is either eternal or temporal. Eternal punishment (Hell) is removed in confession, but temporal punishment remains. This language can be misleading. This is not a punishment from God. It's not as if God says, "Because you did this you deserve 10 years in purgatory unless you make up for it now." The "punishment" is "due to sin." In other words, sin itself imposes a punishment upon us. What is that punishment? It's <u>attachment</u> to sin. By sinning we become attached to the sin through our habit and this attachment is a punishment from the sin itself. God wants to break that attachment. The grace of an indulgence is specifically for this purpose.

**Prescribed Actions of the Church:** All grace comes from God, but the Church is given the authority to dispense the grace of God through certain means. An indulgence is one of those means. Therefore, when the Church says that certain actions open the warehouse of grace, we can be certain that this is true. For example, one of the indulgences offered by the Church requires the following: Make a holy hour before the Blessed Sacrament, go to confession within seven days of that holy hour, receive communion within seven days, and pray for the pope. Upon the completion of these requirements we can be certain that all the grace we need to completely detach from the sins we confess is given to us. That's right. The grace is there.

**Interior Disposition**: But there is one catch to the above explanation! We have to be open to that grace if it is going to have an effect in our lives. And this is the most important part to remember (and the most difficult to fulfill). To illustrate, let's go back to our earlier example. Say a person went to confession, completed the requirements of a full indulgence, and THEN walked outside and was hit by a car and died. Does the indulgence mean the person went straight to Heaven? Maybe, but probably not. The person would go straight to Heaven, bypassing Purgatory, if, and only if, that person's heart was ALSO perfectly open to the infinite grace given through this indulgence. Forgiveness of sin is certain. Therefore, Heaven will happen. But whether one goes to Purgatory or not depends on how open the person is to completely detaching from all sin and all tendency to sin. This is the grace the indulgence seeks to give if we are willing to receive it. And if we do fully open our heart to it, this means we have completely converted to God and are perfectly in His grace. This, of course, must be our goal!

**Types of Indulgences:** An indulgence is either "partial" or "full." "Partial" meaning some of the grace needed for the full conversion is given, and "full" meaning that all of the grace needed is made available if the person's heart is fully open.

So this is the glorious and transforming Sacrament of Penance, Reconciliation, Confession, and Forgiveness. It's a gift so many fear, but a gift we ought to love. Examine your approach to this sacrament and let God speak to you, draw you to it and help you fall in love with it. If you do, you'll find that this is one of the best ways available to encounter the love and mercy of our perfectly loving and merciful God!

# 7

# THE SACRAMENT OF
# ANOINTING OF THE SICK

They drove out many demons, and they anointed with oil many
who were sick and cured them. (Mark 6:13)

Is anyone among you sick? He should summon the presbyters of
the church, and they should pray over him and anoint [him] with oil
in the name of the Lord, and the prayer of faith will save the sick
person, and the Lord will raise him up. If he has committed any
sins, he will be forgiven. (James 5:14-15)

These Scripture verses reveal the foundation for the Sacrament of the
Anointing of the Sick. Furthermore, we can find numerous passages
in the Gospels where Jesus Himself cured the sick and showed
compassion toward them. Jesus loves those who are suffering from
illness, as well as all forms of suffering, in a very direct way. He is
concerned and wants to be present in that suffering. He wants to
bring healing and hope!

Below is the introductory passage from the *Catechism* on Anointing:

"By the sacred anointing of the sick and the prayer of the priests the
whole Church commends those who are ill to the suffering and
glorified Lord, that he may raise them up and save them. And
indeed she exhorts them to contribute to the good of the People of
God by freely uniting themselves to the Passion and death of
Christ" (LG 11; cf. Jas 5:14-16; Rom 8:17; Col 1:24; 2 Tim 2:11-12;
1 Pet 4:13). (#1499)

The best place to start so as to gain a good understanding of this
sacrament is the problem it addresses. It addresses human suffering
due to illness.

Let's ponder the reality of illness and suffering to set the stage for Jesus' answer to it.

## The Suffering of Illness

The *Catechism* states that illness is among the "gravest problems confronted in human life" (#1500). With illness comes various experiences. Let's look at some of them:

**Powerlessness, Limitation, Finitude**: When one is ill, especially seriously ill, there can be an experience of human weakness, vulnerability and powerlessness like never before. Suddenly, the person may be limited to bed, or a hospital, and this experience changes everything that made up normal daily life. When you cannot go about your normal daily life, you find that you are suddenly dependent upon others in a way you have never been before. This vulnerability can either be the cause for anger and despair, or deeper surrender to God and reliance upon the love and care of others.

**Glimpse of Death**: Certainly, not every serious illness will end in death; but every serious illness can give us a glimpse of our mortality. Many of us do not think much about dying. It's as if it is something that is far in the future and not relevant to us at this time in our life. But illness can suddenly lead us to face our human mortality and cause us to look at life in a whole new way.

**Anguish, Self-absorption, Despair and Revolt Against God**: When one experiences a serious illness, there are many temptations present. Physical pain can cause interior anguish. The experience of loss is real and that loss hurts. As a result, those with a serious illness are often tempted to become self-absorbed. And who can blame them? It's hard to think about others when you are experiencing pain and weakness. The tendency is to become focused upon that pain to a point that it leads to despair. Despair is one of the darkest experiences we can go through. It's a loss of hope and trust in God. It produces a deep interior darkness and leaves one desiring a way out. And, at times, this deep interior pain can cause one to question God and His goodness. The classic question is, "How can an all-powerful and all-loving God allow me to go through this?" As a result, there are some who turn from God in anger and revolt.

**Christian Maturity**: But illness does not have to end in despair, anger or revolt against God. There are many who allow the suffering they endure to deepen their faith and make them stronger in their Christian life. Illness forces one to move from mediocrity to a choice to either grow stronger in virtue, trust and goodness, or to turn inward, away from God and others. The hope for any illness or any suffering we endure is that it brings us to a greater reliance on God and a deeper faith. Suffering and illness have great potential to make us much stronger in our character, holiness and virtue. Make sure you let any suffering you endure do just that.

**Search and Return to God**: The ultimate "blessing" that can come from illness is a search for and return to God. Many people of faith have found that, in a moment of grave illness, their faith was strengthened and their love increased. Suddenly, the many idols and "things" of this world seem of little importance. Instead, illness can have the effect of reprioritizing life and focusing in on what is important and on what is eternal. "You can't take it with you" as the saying goes. So the suffering of illness can be a great blessing in disguise when it evokes a return to God and Christian virtue.

What we have to remember, above all else, when one encounters a serious illness, is that Christ is the Great Physician. He always has and always will have the greatest compassion toward those who are ill. We see this so clearly in the Gospels through the many healings Jesus performed. And though Jesus does not always heal physically, He does always heal spiritually. He always acts as the Divine Physician of our souls.

## Who Can Be Anointed By Whom?

Some sacraments can be administered by those who are not priests. For example, deacons can witness marriages and administer baptism. In fact, laity can do the same under special conditions. But most sacraments are reserved to priests and bishops by virtue of the special grace of their ordination. Anointing of the Sick is one of those sacraments which can only be administered by a priest or bishop. And normally, the oil that is used is blessed by the bishop on Holy Thursday and distributed to all the priests of his diocese for use until the following Holy Thursday.

The Sacrament of Anointing is not for the ordinary struggles and weaknesses of daily life. The Sacraments of Confession and the Eucharist are for these daily needs. Anointing of the Sick is specifically for those who, as a result of some serious illness, face the possibility of death. This is a very general definition so let's look at some practical examples.

**Danger of Death**: As mentioned above, every serious illness can offer a glimpse of death, even if death is unlikely. The Sacrament of Anointing is to be given to those who in any way are in danger of death due to an illness. This could be the person going in for surgery, even if it's somewhat routine. Or it could be administered to just about anyone who has been admitted to a hospital for an illness. The guiding principle is to be cautious and generous with the grace of this sacrament. Even if there is only a small possibility of death, it's wise to be anointed.

Of course common sense should come into play. For example, if you have a common cold, you should not be anointed. However, if there are other serious complications which cause the common cold, according to the doctor, to possess some serious risk to you, then you should be anointed.

**At the Beginning of an Illness:** Sometimes it is thought that one should wait until the moment of death to call the priest for anointing. This is a mistake. Anointing should be given at the beginning of a serious illness so that the grace of that sacrament can assist throughout. If, however, the person is anointed at the beginning of a serious illness, and then becomes worse, it is appropriate to anoint again, including when the person is near death.

**Elderly:** When one's "frailty becomes more pronounced" due to advancement in years, the time to anoint has arrived. In this case, the elderly can be anointed on a regular basis as long as their frailty and weakness continues. Some suggest that once a month would be ideal. Those entrusted to the care of a nursing home are ideal candidates for regularly receiving the Anointing of the Sick. Old age is not an illness, but, as we will see later in this chapter, the elderly most certainly are candidates for anointing given their needs, physical weakness, suffering, ailments, and proximity to the end of their lives.

**Mental Illness**: Mental illness brings with it unique challenges and sufferings. As a general rule, those who suffer from some form of mental illness or another serious mental anguish can be anointed. Mental illness can be life threatening at times for a variety of reasons. Anointing should be used with caution though. Just having a bad day, or being particularly down is not a reason for anointing. Minor illness is not a sufficient reason either. Sometimes people seek healing in a general way or in a spiritual way such as from some past struggle or hurt. Again, this is not what this sacrament is for. The Eucharist and Confession offer the grace needed for this type of healing. Discernment on the part of the priest will help in deciding if the person is in need of anointing. So if there is a question about it, speak to your parish priest and let him decide.

The bottom line is that the Sacrament of Anointing should be given generously to those who are in need. If in doubt, it's probably best to anoint. And it's best to do it sooner rather than later. The fact that God made Anointing of the Sick a sacrament tells us that He has a special concern for those who are ill or weakened and wants to pour forth His grace upon them.

**Effects of the Sacrament**

The Sacrament of Anointing has powerful effects, but perhaps some of them are not what we initially expect. We most likely think the purpose of anointing is to ask for a physical healing. That may be the result, but it may not be. This section will present the various effects of this sacrament. Reflecting upon them will especially help us see illness and human suffering the way God sees it. These effects are outlined in the *Catechism* #1532. The various added emphases below (underlined words) highlight some of the specific effects of this sacrament.

**The uniting of the sick person to the passion of Christ, for his own good <u>and</u> that of the whole Church:** This is key to understand and live. It's the great and wonderful mystery of "Redemptive Suffering." So often when we suffer we fall into the trap of thinking that it's bad for us. We can even fall into the trap of thinking that God must not care. But this is simply not the case. The fact of the matter is that Jesus set for us the perfect example of the value of suffering. He endured the greatest of suffering in His life and He did it for a reason. What is this reason? It's twofold: First of all, suffering, illness and death were introduced into this world and our lives as a result of original sin. God's answer was to send His Son into the world to transform death, illness, and all forms of suffering. He transformed it by making it the very means of our eternal salvation. Secondly, He invites us to unite our own sufferings to His so that our suffering can share in His redemptive power. This is glorious and is so often missed. It means that our suffering can have great power and can become a wonderful instrument of grace in our world if we but unite it willingly, freely and joyfully to Christ's. Our suffering, in this way, becomes like a prayer. It takes on meaning and value. In a sense, we can say that our suffering becomes "divinized."

The Sacrament of Anointing offers a special grace to those who are anointed which enables them to more fully unite their suffering to Christ. This will affect their lives greatly, but it will also benefit the entire Church! St. Paul spoke of this when he said, "Now I rejoice in my sufferings for your sake, and in my flesh I am filling up what is lacking in the afflictions of Christ on behalf of his body, which is the church" (Colossians 1:24). Jesus invites us to share not only in His sufferings, but also to share in the redemptive power those sufferings can take on as a result of His Cross.

Those who are anointed should anticipate this grace in a special way and are invited to make a very conscious gift of their sufferings to Christ for their own good and for the good of the entire world.

**The strengthening, peace, and courage to endure in a Christian manner the sufferings of illness or old age:** Suffering is not an end in itself. It is now a means to become closer to Christ. In order to fully unite our sufferings to Christ, we need strength, peace and courage. The Anointing of the Sick offers us that grace.

Patient endurance is very inspiring to those who witness it. Those who suffer much but retain an aura of peace and strength are an inspiration. The suffering isn't inspiring, the strength and peace are. This is also true of those who are frail due to old age. It's easy for the elderly to think that their life is at an end and that it would be better to simply die. Though such thinking is understandable, it would be a mistake to miss the fact that God wants the elderly to offer a special witness to His strength and courage. They do have a mission in life even while in a nursing home or in the hospital. Their witness is greatly needed and is a source of grace to many.

**The <u>forgiveness</u> of sins, <u>if</u> the sick person was not able to obtain it through the Sacrament of Penance:** Often times, when a serious illness or tragedy befalls a person, they do not have time to go to confession. This is obviously the case when they suddenly fall unconscious. In that case, as long as the person to be anointed would have wanted to go to confession, all of their sins are forgiven. God is not picky. He does not say, "Sorry, you missed your opportunity for forgiveness because you were unconscious." No, God's mercy is great and He freely gives forgiveness of sins if it is desired. And God knows our heart so He knows whether we would have desired it and chosen it.

This grace of sacramental forgiveness is an incredible blessing especially at the time of death when the person is unconscious. First and foremost, it's a blessing to the one receiving the Sacrament. But it is also a great consolation to the family members in that they are reassured that God is fully present to their loved ones offering mercy and forgiveness.

**The restoration of health, <u>if it is conducive to the salvation of his soul</u>:** This is a sort of tricky effect you might say. Often times, we pray for healing and expect that the Sacrament of Anointing is primarily for that purpose. But the key language is that healing will take place <u>if</u>, and <u>only if</u>, "it is conducive to the salvation of his soul." Of course, only God knows this so it requires we enter into trust. But what is important to remember is that the ultimate goal in life is salvation! Death is not the end, Heaven is. When we understand this, we will also be faced with the great mystery when God takes a person from this world even if it seems to be before his/her time. Death is a mystery and we are called to trust and surrender to God even when we do not understand His ways.

So what should we pray for when a loved one is close to death and is anointed? The ideal prayer is simply a prayer of entrustment to God. Entrust your loved one, or yourself in your own illness, and believe that God knows best and will provide the grace necessary to achieve what is best.

**The <u>preparation</u> for passing over to eternal life:**  Lastly, it's important to note that this sacrament prepares the soul for the grace of a holy death.  God knows what the soul needs at the moment of death.  Therefore, whatever that soul needs most, God will offer in a way that they are free to receive or reject.  Again, Heaven is our goal and we must never forget that!

In the past, it was common to call the Sacrament of Anointing the "Last Rites" or "Extreme Unction."  This emphasized this "just before death" aspect of the anointing.  And though it is proper at the moment of death, it is now more commonly referred to as Anointing of the Sick so as to emphasize the importance of receiving it not only at the point of death, but also at the beginning, and throughout, an illness.

Ideally, at the point of death the Holy Eucharist should also be given under the form of Viaticum.  Viaticum is simply receiving Jesus in the Eucharist with certain prayers that emphasize that this reception of the Eucharist is for the final journey to Heaven.  "Viaticum" means, "for the journey."

It's worth noting here that the Sacraments for the beginning of the Christian journey are Baptism, Confirmation and Holy Eucharist.  The Sacraments for the final journey are Penance, Anointing and, once again, the Holy Eucharist.

### How and When it is Offered

The Sacrament of Anointing can be offered at any time and in any place.  It can be offered in a home, in a hospital, at a nursing home, at church, or wherever the sick person is.  The Sacrament can come to them.

Practically speaking, if you are going in for surgery it's a good idea to stop by the parish church the day before to be anointed.  Perhaps just call ahead and make an appointment.  Some priests are even able to offer anointing in between Sunday Masses to those who ask.

If someone is suddenly admitted to a hospital and is in critical condition, tell the nursing staff you want a priest to come.  The nursing staff should know how to contact the local priest quickly. For those who are elderly, it's helpful if either the elderly person or a caretaker keep the local parish informed of his/her health and request anointing from time to time. When the elderly person is in a nursing home, anointing may already be offered each month so inquire about it at the local parish.

The bottom line is that you should make sure you seek out this sacrament. Talk to the local parish priest and let him guide you or your loved one on when and how to receive this grace.

# 8

# THE SACRAMENT OF HOLY ORDERS

One of the most important keys to understanding the Sacrament of Holy Orders is to first understand the mission of Christ. Understanding how Jesus entrusted His mission to the Apostles, and to all the faithful, each in their own unique way, will help us deepen our knowledge of the Sacrament of Holy Orders.

## The Mission of Christ

Let's start with some questions. What was the mission of Christ? What did He come to do on Earth? The best way to answer these questions is to examine all that pointed to His coming in the Old Testament. There we see what we call "prefigurations" of Christ. These are people, words and actions by which God prepared to come to Earth to fulfill His mission. Specifically, we can identify three prefigurations that God offered in the Old Testament that are fulfilled in the mission of Christ: 1) The Levitical Priests; 2) The Prophets; 3) And the Kings.

**Levitical Priests:** From the beginning of time, after the fall of Adam and Eve, God invited humanity to begin a process of atoning for sin. Cain and Abel were the first to bring animal sacrifices to God (Genesis 4:3-5). Abel's was acceptable to God since it was the firstborn of his flock. After that, Noah offered sacrifice to God (Genesis 8:20-21). And who could forget the sacrifice of Abraham (Genesis 22)? God called him to offer his firstborn son, Isaac, but stopped him just before the sacrifice, allowing him to offer a ram instead.

Eventually, God formed the people of Israel and led them forth from slavery in Egypt by Moses and Aaron. The gift of freedom from slavery in Egypt was instituted by the first Passover. God had Moses and Aaron instruct the people:

> Tell the whole community of Israel: On the tenth of this month every family must procure for itself a lamb, one apiece for each household. If a household is too small for a lamb, it along with its nearest neighbor will procure one, and apportion the lamb's cost in proportion to the number of persons, according to what each household consumes. Your lamb must be a year-old male and without blemish. You may take it from either the sheep or the goats. You will keep it until the fourteenth day of this month, and then, with the whole community of Israel assembled, it will be slaughtered during the evening twilight. They will take some of its blood and apply it to the two doorposts and the lintel of the houses in which they eat it. (Exodus 12:3-7).

Every house offered an animal sacrifice, sprinkled blood on the door post, and prepared to be set free. Then, many years later, once settled in the new Promised Land of Israel, God formed the Levitical Priesthood from the descendents of Aaron. God laid down various instructions (found in Exodus and especially the Book of Leviticus) which guided the Levitical priests in their duty of offering sacrifice. Solomon built the first temple which was dedicated to sacrifice. Animal sacrifice continued until after the time of Christ, when the second temple was destroyed in 70 A.D., never to be rebuilt.

Without going into an exhaustive study of the Levitical Priesthood, suffice it to say that these priests, as with all those before them who offered sacrifice to God, were prefigurations of the one High Priest, Jesus Christ, who offered Himself as the perfect and spotless Lamb of God, the firstborn Son, to atone for the sins of the world. Jesus was the final and ultimate Priest who offered Himself as the final and ultimate Sacrifice.

**Prophets:** Other prefigurations of Christ in the Old Testament were the Prophets. They were called by God, and anointed with the Holy Spirit, to speak God's message. It was typically a message of repentance and conversion by which God continually called His straying people back to Himself. The prophets were men of God (1 Samuel 2:27), servants and messengers of the Lord (Isaiah 42:19), seers (Isaiah 30:10), filled with the Spirit (Hosea 9:7), and watchmen for the people (Ezekiel 3:17).

There were formal prophets designated by God and anointed for that role, and those not formally given the title but who, nonetheless, acted as God's messengers. Abraham was called a prophet (spokesman) by God in Genesis 20:7. Aaron was a spokesman of Moses who was a messenger of God in Exodus 7:1.

The best known formal prophets are Isaiah, Jeremiah, Ezekiel and Daniel since much is written down about them. They are referred to as the Major Prophets. There are also twelve Minor Prophets: Hosea, Amos, Micah, Zephaniah, Haggai, Zechariah, Joel, Obadiah, Jonah, Nauum, Habakkuk, and Malachi. In addition, Joshua was referred to as a prophet as was Samuel. Joshua succeeded Moses and led the people into the Promised Land, and Samuel was the last of those referred to as the Judges.

As with the section on the priesthood above, we could go into great detail regarding the Old Testament prophets, their works, and the uniqueness of each of their situations. But that is not the purpose of this current chapter. Instead, the goal is to illustrate that prophets played a significant role prior to Christ preparing the people for the coming of the Messiah in various ways. Most specifically, they continually spoke for God and called the people back to God from their evil ways. They spoke the truths of God and were inspired by God to do so.

The greatest of the Old Testament Prophets is actually found in the New Testament. John the Baptist is the greatest and last of the Old Testament Prophets because he was the immediate precursor to Christ. He prepared the way for His immediate coming.

Jesus takes on this new role of the Prophet of all prophets by coming as Truth itself. He is the Truth, the Way and the Life. He is the Word of God in fullness. He is the definitive and final "statement" from God revealing all truth. Jesus is the fulfillment of all Prophets.

**King**: In our day and age we tend to separate civil governance from the Church. The "Separation of Church and State" we say. As a result, we can fall into the trap of thinking this means separation of God and civil governance. But is this what God intended? Is this the way it has always been and is it the way it will always be? The answer is no, no and no. In creating the world, God intended to be centrally involved in its governance. And He will do just that in eternity when He establishes the new Heavens and new Earth.

In the Old Testament we see God raising up leaders to govern. Noah, Abraham and Moses led their people with the authority of governance. Saul, David and Solomon were known as powerful kings. And there were numerous other kings who were anointed and empowered by God to rule His people.

The role of a king was ultimately to govern in truth and justice, respecting and implementing God's law as the ultimate law. King David, especially, was seen as a good king who governed with a shepherd's heart. Though he wasn't perfect, he brought stability and peace to God's people.

Throughout the Old Testament we see God shepherding his people with good leaders. But we also see leaders who go astray and wreak havoc on the community.

But all of these leaders were only prefigurations of the one great Leader, Shepherd and Ruler to come. And that, of course, is the King of Kings...Jesus. Jesus, as King, came to be the perfect Shepherd of all. His kingship is one that governs the spiritual world now, and at the end of time, He will rule the material world in perfect justice. He governs our souls as we let Him and desires to bring perfect order and peace. He is the perfect King.

So the point of this section was to illustrate the mission of Christ. He was sent by the Father, into the world, to be Priest, Prophet and King. In fact, He was the perfect fulfillment of each one of these roles. Together, they sum up His entire mission.

From here, let's look at how Jesus entrusted His mission to the Apostles as well as His entire Body, the Church.

## Entrusting the Mission

Jesus is no longer here on Earth, or is He? As mentioned in the chapter on Penance, after His resurrection, Jesus appeared to the Apostles as they were locked in the upper room:

[Jesus] said to them again, "Peace be with you. As the Father has sent me, so I send you." And when he had said this, he breathed on them and said to them, "Receive the holy Spirit." (John 20:21-22)

There are two key parts to this passage. First, Jesus said, "As the Father has sent me, so I send you." This is key because it shows that the Apostles were to now share in the very mission of Christ. They were to share in the mission that Jesus was sent to fulfill by the Father. They were being sent, as Jesus Himself said earlier in John's Gospel, to do even greater works than He did (see John 14:12-14). So this tells us clearly that Jesus' mission to be Priest, Prophet and King did not end with His ascension into Heaven. In fact, His earthly life was, in some ways, just the beginning of His mission.

The second key part in this passage is the gift of the Holy Spirit, "And when He had said this, He breathed on them and said to them, 'Receive the Holy Spirit.'" It is by a unique gift of the Holy Spirit, namely, ordination to Holy Orders, that the Apostles are now able to carry out Jesus' mission as Priest, Prophet and King. It is not by their own effort or power they carry out the mission.

Of course, the Apostles were not the only ones entrusted with the mission of Christ. By virtue of our Baptism and Confirmation, all the faithful, that is, the entire Body of Christ is entrusted with this threefold mission of Christ. Ordained ministers fulfill this threefold mission in a very unique way that is different than the laity who share in the mission of Christ through a participation called the "Royal Priesthood."

Here are some examples of how the laity fulfill the threefold mission of Christ:

**Priestly Role:**
- Offering their life to Christ as a living sacrifice
- Offering their daily work to Christ that He may sanctify it
- Offering of prayers to Christ so that He may sanctify the world
- Offering works of charity to Christ as a sacrifice of love for others

**Prophetic Role:**
- Spreading the Word of God in the world
- Prophetic witness through a life of virtue
- Catechetical teaching roles within the Church
- Parents teaching their children the faith

**Kingly Role:**
- Allowing Christ to govern their own soul so that their soul lives in God's Kingdom
- Ordering civil society to bring all laws into conformity with the divine law
- Impacting culture so that it reflects the truths of God
- Parents fulfill this role by guiding their children and helping them to live lives in conformity to Christ's

With this basic understanding of the role the laity play in fulfilling the mission of Christ, let's now turn our attention to the way the ordained fulfill this mission in their unique way. In order to understand this properly, we must understand, first, the three degrees of Sacred Ordination: bishop, priest and deacon.

### The Degrees of Ordination

**Episcopacy (bishops):** The bishops are the successors to the Apostles. A little known fact is that every bishop actually could trace his line of ordination back to the Apostles. Of course this may be impossible to do for most bishops, practically speaking, in that it would be hard to find the historical records of ordination all the way back. But it is true that every bishop is directly descended from the Apostles. From that upper room, when the Apostles were ordained by Christ, they eventually went out to evangelize and govern the world. As they established a new Christian community, an Apostle would ordain a new bishop to care for that new church. Those new bishops would do the same and so forth until today. This unbroken chain of ordination is essential to a bishop's valid ordination. Without it, there would be the complete loss of the episcopacy as well as the priesthood and deaconate.

Being the direct descendents of the Apostles, bishops share in the fullness of the priesthood. Only they have the authority to ordain new priests and deacons. The Holy Father in Rome, the pope, is a bishop also. Being the successor of St. Peter himself, he exercises a singular spiritual authority over the entire Church. But in regard to his ordination, the pope is no more or less a bishop than every other bishop.

**Presbyters (Priests):** Like the bishops, presbyters share in the priesthood of Christ. They exercise the same spiritual power to celebrate Mass, forgive sins, bring healing, preach with authority and shepherd souls. The difference is that priests are tied to a bishop. They are coworkers with the bishop in the ministry of Christ. In fact, every priest must be under a bishop to function in his role. Even those in religious orders must be tied either to the local bishop, or to the pope himself, as their bishop.

**Deacons:** Deacons are not ordained to the priesthood; rather, they are ordained "unto the ministry." This ministry is one of service in the Church. They do not take on the role of shepherd in the same way priests and bishop do, but they are entrusted with the task of preaching with authority. They also must be tied to a bishop and act as servants in the Church in their own unique way according to the needs of the Church.


## Fulfilling Christ's Mission through Ordination

Let's now look at how the threefold mission of Christ, of priest, prophet and king, is fulfilled in the ordained minister. We already looked at how these roles are fulfilled in the laity through the royal priesthood, so it is now important to understand how they are fulfilled through ordained ministry.

**Priestly Role:** As mentioned, presbyters and bishops share in Christ's priesthood in a unique way by virtue of their ordination. This unique participation differs from that of the laity and deacons not only in degree, but in essence. In other words, it's not that presbyters and bishops just fulfill this role to a greater degree as if supercharged; rather, they fulfill this role in an entirely different way.

Presbyters and bishops fulfill the priestly role of Christ by actually perpetuating the one and eternal Sacrifice of the Cross through the offering of the Holy Eucharist. As the priest offers Mass, it is Christ Himself who is present offering the one eternal Sacrifice. We say that the priest acts *in Persona Christi*, that is, "in the Person of Christ." So it is not the priest himself offering the Mass; rather, it is Christ who is alive in and one with the priest. By virtue of the priest's ordination, it is Christ Himself who offers each Mass.

Presbyters and bishops also act *in Persona Christi* every time they absolve sins in the confessional and every time they anoint a person with the oil of the sick in the Sacrament of Anointing.

This sharing in the mission of Christ is "priestly" because its source is the grace of the one perfect Sacrifice of the Cross, which was Jesus' perfect priestly act.

**Prophetic Role:** All people are called to share the Word of God by what they say and what they do. That includes priests, laity, and religious. But each one does it in their own unique way. Those who share in the ordained ministry share in the prophetic mission of Christ in a powerful way.

Let's look at a practical example to help illustrate this point. Say there is a layman who gives a class at a local parish on the Gospel of John. What he shares is good, true and insightful. Now imagine that this same talk is given by the parish priest. The content is the same, the words are the same, but is the prophetic message the same? The answer is that, even though what is said is the same, the fact that the priest gives the message is significant. By virtue of his ordination, the message he speaks takes on an added authority. God speaks not only through the priest's words, but also through his sacred ministry. And, of course, the same is true if what is taught is erroneous. In that case, the error taught by someone ordained is more damaging to the Church than if it were taught by someone not ordained.

The point of this illustration is to show that God speaks His Word through the ordained ministry in a unique and powerful way. God's Word is not just words, rather, His Word is a communication of His very Person.

This is especially true within the sacred Liturgy itself. The Liturgy is a sacred action of both Christ and the Church. Jesus shows up sacramentally, but He also shows up as the Word that is proclaimed. For that reason, the ordained minister is the only one who is permitted to preach within the context of the Liturgy. This homily is to be a heart to heart conversation between God and His people, a revealing of the very mind, heart and Person of God Himself. And the glorious truth is that God is able to accomplish this revealing of Himself through the ordained minister despite the fact that the ordained minister is a sinner like the rest of humanity. God can do amazing things even with poor instruments.

By analogy, it would be like a master musician who picks up an inexpensive violin and produces beautiful music. Sure, the better the instrument the better the sound. But, more important than a good instrument is the musician himself. God is that Musician and we are the instrument. He uses us, and in the case of the Liturgy, uses the ordained minister as a means of His glorious Word.

The bishops (and especially the pope, as explained in Book One of this series) are entrusted with the fullness of the proclamation of the Word of God. Priests also share in this ministry of the Word as coworkers of the bishops. Deacons are also entrusted with the proclamation of the Word of God by virtue of their ordination and are also given a special gift (charism) so as to preach that Word with authority.

**Kingly Role:** Too often we have a misunderstanding of what it means to be a "king" or to act with the authority of governance. Our common misunderstanding of this role seems to stem from the fact that so many, throughout history, have abused their power of governance. This is seen in numerous forms of abuse found in secular governance throughout the ages. It is also found in abuses of authority within the Church itself. There is an old phrase that comes to mind here, "absolute power corrupts absolutely." Though this may not always be the case, it is a common tendency due to our fallen human nature. The power of governance of people brings with it temptations to abuse that authority and to govern with harshness and selfishness.

Jesus' Kingship was of the highest order and is the perfect model for all governance. He ruled like a shepherd, humbly leading His sheep, keeping them safe and feeding them. The shepherd is intimately involved in the day to day life of the sheep. He is there in the sheepfold with them. They know the shepherd, hear his voice and follow him.

Priests and bishops are empowered by virtue of their ordination to act as shepherds to God's people in the very name and person of Christ. This priestly governance (also referred to as "hierarchy" – hieros=priestly and arch=governance) is manifested in two primary ways. First, it's manifested in the external governance of the Church itself, and, secondly, it's manifested in a more personal shepherding of individual souls.

The priestly governance of the Church is exercised on various levels. The pope is entrusted with the universal governance of the whole Church on Earth. Each bishop is entrusted with the governance of his local church (diocese). And priests, when given the responsibility of being a Pastor, are entrusted with the governance of their parish. This governance brings with it various rights and responsibilities and is exercised, ideally, with the heart of Christ.

On a more personal, one-on-one level, all priests and bishops are entrusted with the care of souls and are called to shepherd people through their pastoral ministry. This certainly includes offering them the Sacraments and preaching the Word of God, but it also includes individual shepherding through spiritual guidance. This more intimate encounter between God's people and priests reveals the personal nature of shepherding. Shepherding (governance) is not at all just about the priest "being in charge;" rather, it's first and foremost about the priest or bishop leading God's people to Christ.

**Some Practical Considerations**

The previous pages of this chapter give a general understanding of Holy Orders, its origin in the Old Testament, its fulfillment in Christ, and Christ's entrustment of that mission to the Church. In addition to this general overview of Holy Orders, it is important that we look at several practical considerations and questions that often come up.

Let's look at why Holy Orders is reserved only to men, celibacy, the distinction between religious and diocesan priests, and how ordination itself takes place.

**Ordination of Men:** The ordination of bishops, priests and deacons is reserved only to men. Why is that? Is it a form of discrimination? Is it a hold out from the past? Will it ever change? These are important questions to properly understand and answer.

The answer to these questions is quite simple. The reason only men are ordained is because we do what Jesus did. Jesus was male. God the Son took on human flesh in the form of a man. Jesus picked twelve men as His Apostles and they became His first bishops. Also, from that time on, those whom the Apostles picked as their successors and coworkers were men. Therefore, the Church continues to do what Jesus and the Apostles did.

The same is true of the deaconate. In Acts 6 we have the institution of the deaconate. The Apostles needed help and they chose seven men to be ordained deacons. This practice then continued on throughout the centuries.

What's key to understand here is that, with all of the Sacraments, we do what Jesus did. For example, we baptize with water because Jesus was baptized with water. We use bread and wine for the Mass because that's what Jesus did. And we use men for ordination because that's what Jesus did.

It's easy to question this and wonder why Jesus picked only men for His first bishops. Was it just the cultural influences of the time? Was Jesus Himself pressured by that culture? No, certainly not. Jesus was very often counter-cultural and not afraid to stand up to the erroneous practices of the time. So we should conclude that He did what He freely willed to do.

Another question that may arise is whether this means Jesus, or the Church, is prejudiced by restricting ordination only to men. Again, most certainly not. There is nothing wrong in choosing only men for ordination. Truthfully, we will only fully know why Jesus did this when we get to Heaven. We'll have to ask Him then. But we should know and believe that Jesus was not prejudiced. In fact, He was quite caring and counter-cultural in the way He treated women with the utmost respect and dignity. But, for some reason, he chose men for Holy Orders. In our day and age we tend to think that equality of dignity means sameness of roles and responsibilities. But is that true? What is true is that men and women are 100% equal in dignity, but differ in their roles in the world, family and the Church. We must be very careful not to fall into the trap of thinking that being "different" implies being "better" or "worse." It doesn't. We should not be afraid to embrace the difference between men and women in accord with God's plan, while maintaining complete equality in dignity.

Can this practice of ordaining only men ever change? No, it cannot change anymore than the Church could change using bread and wine for Mass or water for Baptism. So this practice will remain until the end of time.

**Celibacy**: In the Western Church the practice of ordaining only celibate priests and bishops is the norm. A Married man can be ordained a deacon, but if his wife were to pass away before he does, he cannot remarry.

In the Eastern Church the practice of priestly celibacy is optional, therefore, married men can be ordained. However, bishops are chosen only from those priests who choose to live celibacy.

Why do we have celibacy in the Western Church? This could be answered from varying perspectives. Scripturally, Jesus himself spoke of those who would remain celibate for the sake of the Kingdom (Matthew 19:12). And we should not forget that Jesus Himself was celibate. St. Paul speaks of celibacy as an ideal in 1 Corinthians 7. And as the Apostles went forth to proclaim the Gospel to new towns and countries, they left their families behind to fulfill their missions.

As for "why" we have celibacy, it seems that, in addition to its Scriptural basis and the witness of Christ as a celibate, there are practical, ministerial, and symbolic reasons.

Practically speaking, celibacy allows a priest to fully dedicate himself to His priestly ministry. And this is the ideal for a priest. If a priest were married with children, it would be only proper that his wife and children would take precedence over his priestly ministry. However, a priest must strive to imitate Christ in every way. Priests must, ideally, make their priestly ministry the center of their lives. For that reason, married priests will more easily experience a certain conflict between two very good things – their ministry and their family. Not that this would be an irreconcilable conflict or even a negative conflict. It would simply be a conflict of priorities. Therefore, the Western Church has maintained celibacy so that priests can be singly focused on their ministry.

Could celibacy ever change? Theologically speaking, yes it could. The pope has the authority to change this since it is a discipline of the Church and not an essential part of the priestly ministry. After all, some of the Apostles were married, priests in the Eastern Church can be married, and there are even extreme situations within the Western Church when priests can be married. (When a married Anglican priest converts to Catholicism he can get permission to be ordained a Catholic priest while still being married.) However, though celibacy *could* change in theory, most believe it will not change. It's been the practice for many centuries, has been one of the core reasons for the Church's missionary impulse, and will most likely remain the practice of the Church.

**Religious and Diocesan Priests**: The first thing that should be said about the distinction between religious order priests and diocesan priests is that a priest is a priest. There are not two forms of the priesthood. All priests are priests, all deacons are deacons, and all bishops are bishops. However, there are different ways that priests live out their priestly ministry. One of the primary distinctions is whether they are religious or diocesan priests.

A religious priest is one who first belongs to a religious order, such as the Franciscans or Dominicans, and later, with the consent of the order's superiors, is also ordained. The primary reason for a religious to also be ordained a priest is to help fulfill the mission of the order. These priests remain religious brothers or monks and exercise their priesthood/deaconate in accord with the direction of the superiors of that order. Religious priests take vows in accord with the practice of their order but most every order takes vows of celibacy, obedience and chastity.

Diocesan priests are ordained for a specific diocese, under a specific bishop, for the purpose to serve its needs. Diocesan priests make solemn promises of obedience and celibacy. Obedience means, first and foremost, that a priest fulfills the ministerial responsibilities assigned to him by his bishop. Celibacy is straight forward in that it means a diocesan priest sacrifices the good of marriage and family for the sake of being singularly devoted to the priestly ministry.

**Ordination Itself**: If you ever have the opportunity to attend a beautiful and solemn ordination ceremony it is worth it. A diocesan priest prepares for ordination through eight years of study after high school. This typically involves an undergraduate degree in philosophy and a graduate degree in theology. During the time of priestly formation, the seminarian also engages in various apostolic ministries, spiritual direction and formation of his human personality. A religious will often also fulfill at least eight years of study and, at times, even more.

Only a bishop can ordain a man to the deaconate or priesthood. Bishops are ordained by other bishops. Customarily this takes place with at least three bishops present.

The ritual involves publically making the priestly and diaconal promises, the laying on of hands and, for priests, anointing of their hands with chrism oil. During the ceremony they are vested in their new liturgical garb and are welcomed by the other priests or deacons present. It is truly a glorious ceremony.

The last thing to mention about ordination is that, like Baptism and Confirmation, Holy Orders imparts an "indelible character" upon the soul of the ordained. This means that once a man is ordained, he is ordained eternally. There is no way to take this sacred gift away. Even if he were to leave or be removed from active ministry, the spiritual character of ordination would not be erased. Once a bishop, priest or deacon, always a bishop, priest or deacon.

We've just scratched the surface of Holy Orders but, hopefully, this basic introduction to this sacrament helps you grow in appreciation for the gift of our bishops, priests and deacons. They are here to serve the Church and rely greatly upon the prayers and support of the laity.

# 9

# THE SACRAMENT OF MATRIMONY

"The matrimonial covenant, by which a man and a woman establish between themselves a partnership of the whole of life, is by its nature ordered toward the good of the spouses and the procreation and education of offspring; this covenant between baptized persons has been raised by Christ the Lord to the dignity of a Sacrament" ( CIC, can. 1055 § 1; cf. GS 48 § 1). (*CCC* #1601)

Marriage is intended to be the most stable institution in every society. For some, it is the most glorious and fulfilling relationship in their lives. Sadly, for others, marriage can leave deep wounds and hurt. This chapter will examine marriage from the design and perspective of God. Though Christian Marriage presents couples with a high ideal, like any gift from God, this ideal requires understanding, love and perseverence. Let's begin with the original intent and design of God.

## God's Design and Intention for Marriage

The first and most fascinating fact about marriage is that God instituted it from the very beginning of the creation of man and woman. It's part of nature. This means that, unlike the other Sacraments, it predates the Sacraments. It has its roots in the "order of nature."

From the very beginning, God meant for male and female to enter into a communion with each other:

God created mankind in his image;
in the image of God he created them;
male and female he created them.

God blessed them and God said to them: Be fertile and multiply; fill the earth and subdue it. Have dominion over the fish of the sea, the birds of the air, and all the living things that crawl on the earth. (Genesis 1:27-28)

The man gave names to all the tame animals, all the birds of the air, and all the wild animals; but none proved to be a helper suited to the man.
So the LORD God cast a deep sleep on the man, and while he was asleep, he took out one of his ribs and closed up its place with flesh. The LORD God then built the rib that he had taken from the man into a woman. When he brought her to the man, the man said:
"This one, at last, is bone of my bones
and flesh of my flesh;
This one shall be called 'woman,'
for out of man this one has been taken."
That is why a man leaves his father and mother and clings to his wife, and the two of them become one body.
The man and his wife were both naked, yet they felt no shame. (Genesis 2:20-25)

These passages from Scripture reveal that man and woman are made for each other, to become united as one in marriage. It's essential that we begin with the "order of nature" to properly understand marriage as part of God's original design.

Being made in the image and likeness of God reveals, among many other things, that people are capable of love and unity. They are capable of giving themselves to another, receiving another, coming to know another, loving another, and, in that mutual love, becoming "fruitful." Of course bearing children and raising a family is one central way that a husband and wife become fruitful. Even those who are not able to bear children are called to bear fruit from their marriage in a life-giving way. "Life-giving" love can manifest itself in a variety of ways, but it will always be the fruit of shared mutual love.

The Book of Genesis reveals that husband and wife are called to "become one body." This oneness is a source of strength and stability for the couple, for any children born of them, and, in fact, for all of society. The unity of marriage is one of the fundamental building blocks of all society.

# The Effect of the Fall

Since marriage was part of the original design of God, and since our first parents sinned and turned from God, marriage itself was deeply affected, as was all of creation. Suddenly, disorder of every type was introduced into married life as a result of sin. Humanity saw "discord, a spirit of domination, infidelity, jealousy, and conflicts" enter into marriage (*CCC* #1606).

The difficulties of marriage as a result of the fall are clear. The ideals of married life are hard to enter into and require continually deepening love and commitment. Sin, hurt, memories of the past, passion and disorder all challenge the natural marriage bond and make it difficult for married couples to live out the glorious vocation of love, unity and fruitfulness they have been called to.

But God did not abandon us nor did He abandon marriage. He has an answer and offers this answer so that this natural institution can reach its fulfillment.

# God's Answer

God saw the effects of the fall of man and, as a result, introduced a glorious plan that affects all aspects of human life and to restore humanity to a new level of communion with Him by the grace of the Sacrifice of His Son. This plan understands marriage as a natural good which was part of God's original intention for humanity.

God's plan was to establish a new covenant with humanity. A covenant could be seen as a form of a contract, but a contract that is elevated to a whole new level. It's not just an exchange of promises, but an exchange of persons. God invites the human race to enter into a new union with Him, a new relationship in which God states, as He did in the Old Testament, "I will take you as my own people, and I will be your God" (Exodus 6:7). God's love for His people in the Old Testament culminated in God giving the Israelites the Ten Commandments through Moses. The Israelites keeping of these Commandments, in turn, expressed their fidelity to God.

However, it became clear that the people of Israel could not always be faithful to this new covenant. Their relationship with God experienced the effects of their sins. But God did not abandon them. He promised to take this covenant to a whole new level. In the Prophets, this covenant moved beyond the law and focused upon a new interior relationship between God and man. For example, Ezekiel 11:19-20 states:

> And I will give them another heart and a new spirit I will put within them. From their bodies I will remove the hearts of stone, and give them hearts of flesh, so that they walk according to my statutes, taking care to keep my ordinances. Thus they will be my people, and I will be their God.

This New Covenant was to be established through the Incarnation of the Son of God and the Sacrifice of His life on the Cross. First, by taking on our human nature, God the Son restores and elevates human nature to a whole new level. Humanity is now "divinized" so to speak. There is a new bond established between God and humanity that is greater than the original bond established at creation.

This new bond is also made possible because God the Son, after taking on human nature, destroyed sin and death by His own death. He destroyed it by entering into the effects of sin (i.e., death), and then by rising to new life. Thus, He restores and elevates human nature to a new resurrected state. As a result of this new life, humanity can now have the heart of Christ live within them. We can now live in Christ and He in us. We are wedded to Him in a new and transforming way.

This bond ultimately becomes a new marital covenant, a marriage of intimate union between God and His people. Jesus becomes the Bridegroom and His people, the Church, become the bride. This New Covenant, the new Divine Marriage, invites consent from each person to enter into an interior union with God. The heart of Christ now consumes and transforms each human heart. We live in Christ and He lives in us.

This reality of the New Covenant is not only the basis of the entire Christian life, it is also now the basis of marriage in Christ. Marriage could not be saved as a purely natural institution. Thus, God elevates all of fallen human nature to a new level. This includes the elevation of the natural order of marriage to the supernatural level of a sacrament. Marriage is now endowed with the spiritual power of the death and resurrection of Christ. This natural bond is elevated by grace to a share in the New Covenant in Christ. What a glorious and awe-inspiring plan our loving God has unfolded for humanity!

## Christian Marriage in the New Covenant

When two baptized people enter into the Covenant of Marriage, this marriage is automatically elevated to the level of a sacrament. As a sacrament, Christian Marriage produces an abundance of good fruit and has new and profound effects upon the couple. Christian Marriage also calls a couple to a new level of self-giving and responsibility. Let's look at some of these effects and good fruits in Christian Marriage.

**Unity:** It's important to acknowledge the inner desire we all have for unity. As humans, we are made for unity, to be in a deep personal communion with one another. And there is no way to erase the longing within our heart for this unity. Husband and wife are called by God to share in a very profound and unique unity, "That the two may become one." For that reason, marriage has the potential to bring about the greatest human fulfillment when that unity is well lived. Of course, discord within marriage produces great hurt since the natural longings of our hearts then go unsatisfied.

As a result of the fall in Genesis, men and women were not, and are not, able to live out this natural call to unity within marriage. Therefore, by bringing marriage into the New Covenant of grace, God bestows a new power on this natural institution infusing it with supernatural grace. Couples are now strengthened, in Christ, to live the unity that Jesus shares with the Father and the love He has for the entire Church. Marriage is now sacramental, shares in this new grace, and enjoys unity among its greatest benefits.

Of course, as with all aspects of the Christian life, couples are not forced to accept this new grace but can freely reject it. And it takes both husband and wife to fully embrace the New Covenant in their marriage for the unity Christ intends to be lived.

**Indissolubility:** Sacramental Marriage creates permanent and lasting unity. Once God makes a promise, He does not go back on it. This permanence provides the necessary foundation for couples to have the stability they need in life and also the necessary context to raise a family if God so blesses a couple with children.

Indissolubility means just that. There is no way around it. A valid Christian marriage cannot be undone. It is "until death do you part." This means that even if a validly married couple were to get civilly divorced, the Church would still consider them married and they would, in fact, still be married. Again, this bond cannot be broken.

Now, you may be wondering about annulments and the fact that there are some who go through a marriage in a Catholic Church, eventually get divorced, receive an annulment from the Church, and then get married again within the Catholic Church. This can be confusing if not properly understood. The section later in this chapter on "Matrimonial Consent" will address this question. But for now, just know that when a couple enters a valid Christian marriage, the bond cannot be broken.

**Fidelity:** Fidelity means that married couples commit themselves to each other exclusively in regards to conjugal love. Fidelity is inherent to the nature of the sexual relationship itself. Sexual love exists for the purpose of unity and childbearing. Childbearing should take place within the context of the committed and permanent relationship of marriage. This is the loving context that God intended children to be born into and nurtured.

But the sexual act also produces profound unity between the couple. In fact, it is this act, along with the vows of marriage, that seals and makes permanent the marriage covenant. In this act, the two become one flesh. Therefore, conjugal love is also spiritual in nature and produces a powerful spiritual bond that must be exercised and experienced only in the context of this life-long permanent covenant of marriage.

The fidelity of married couples also shares in the very fidelity that God has for His people. Christian Marriage stands as a witness to the world of the unwavering fidelity of Christ to the Church. Jesus' New Covenant with humanity is the source of the fidelity of married couples. For that reason, marriage becomes a sign to the world of God's love and commitment.

**Openness to New Life:** An essential commitment married couples make is that of openness to new life. This especially means an openness to children. Of course, not every couple is able to have children due to age or other factors. But the key is the openness. And it's key to understand that this is an "essential" commitment they make. By being essential, if a couple intentionally excludes the possibility of children, they are actually not entering into marriage. More will be said on this in the section on matrimonial consent.

**A Help in Holiness:** Marriage was designed by God because "it is not good for the man to be alone." God, therefore, decided to make a "suitable helpmate" for him. In the ideal of Christian Marriage, spouses are true helpmates for each other on the road to salvation. They image the love of God in that they are to always be there, in good times and bad. They are stable, reliable, concerned, merciful and loving in every way.

Spouses are "helpmates" in countless practical and human ways. They assist each other with daily duties of the home, through shared finances, offer emotional support, they share in each other's joys and sorrows, and are present to all the ordinary parts of human life. However, among the many ways that spouses are helpmates to each other, none is more important than being a helpmate toward holiness. Spouses must regularly assist each other in their relationship with God. They do this by offering the love of God to each other, challenging each other, keeping each other accountable, and experiencing the joys of the Kingdom together. Ideally they pray together and witness their faith to each other. In some cases, one spouse lives his or her faith to a much fuller extent. In that situation, the faithful spouse may be the ticket for the other to Heaven. But, ideally, both act as instruments of the grace of God to each other.

**Mutual Subjection:** One tendency within fallen human nature is to dominate others. Both men and women struggle with this tendency in different ways. We want to be in charge and make the decisions in life and we often want to control others. This tendency, to dominate, is a result of the fall and is sinful. This is especially the case when domination enters into marriage. Throughout history, in many cultures, the primary tendency has been for men to dominate their wives. Many cultures have even treated women as second class citizens. However, wives fall into this same trap of trying to dominate their husbands in their own ways. Often times, this tendency is expressed primarily through the extreme use of emotions.

But regardless of how this tendency to dominate the other is lived out, the solution is the same. The solution is a mutual subjection of husband and wife to each other respecting each other's dignity and unique feminine and masculine roles they each bring to their marriage. Men and women are clearly different in numerous ways, and that is a good thing because that's the way God designed us. Therefore, the unique gifts of masculinity and femininity must be lived and respected in marriage. True masculinity will not be domineering nor will true femininity. Rather, mutual subjection means that each spouse submits to the other in accord with their nature and treats the other with the utmost respect and dignity. Practically speaking, when this mutual submission takes place, neither spouse will be afraid to let the other fulfill their masculine or feminine role within the marriage. The man may make the final decision in a marriage but only after listening to his wife's heart and letting that be their mutual guide. The wife, in this case, will not be afraid to let her husband be the head of the home since she experiences complete respect from him, and her gift of a feminine heart becomes the guiding light for her husband.

Spouses must strive, every day, to discover the way God wants them to live out their love and mutual submission in keeping with their natural gifts and roles. This is hard to do, but must be at the heart of any good and holy marriage. The Sacrament of Matrimony will provide the grace needed to live out this complimentarity of male and female acting together as one.

## Matrimonial Consent

With this explanation of Christian Marriage in the New Covenant, we can now look at matrimonial consent. This consent is what brings about the actual Sacrament of Marriage and produces the wonderful fruits and effects of marriage. Consent is something that must be total and must be free. Force, fear, manipulation pressure and the like undermines the effect of consent and, therefore, undermines marriage itself. On the other hand, consent that is free and total produces the wonderful fruits of marriage outlined in the previous section of this book. Let's look at consent more clearly so as to understand what is needed for consent to bring about a permanent and lasting marriage.

**Free Consent:** The consent that couples offer in marriage must be free. Free consent means that there is nothing present that adds excessive pressure to either person in making the decision to enter into marriage. They should be of sound mind, fully understand the seriousness of their commitment, and make that commitment out of a completely free will decision. Factors that undermine freedom would be pressure, manipulation, fear, immaturity, drugs or alcohol addiction, and the like.

For example, the idea of a "shotgun wedding" illustrates a real danger to free consent. Say a couple ends up getting pregnant out of wedlock. Suddenly, one or both of the persons feels great pressure to get married. Certainly it is entirely possible to make the free choice to get married in this situation for the right reasons. However, if one or both persons decide to get married because they "have to," this is a problem. Choosing to get married out of feelings of pressure undermines marriage itself and could actually lead to the marriage being invalid meaning the bond never actually takes place.

Another example that illustrates a lack of freedom in choosing marriage is that of immaturity. Say, for example, a couple chooses to get married quickly as a result of initial and extreme romantic feelings. They are quite young and immature and do not really understand the depth of commitment they are making. It is possible that their immaturity and emotions cloud their ability to make an authentic and free choice for marriage. The same would be the case of one who attempts to enter into marriage while addicted to drugs and alcohol. Those addictions could so hinder a person's clear thinking that they are incapable of making a free choice on the level necessary for the marriage bond to form.

**Total Consent**: The free consent of couples to enter into marriage must also be total. This means that they must be freely committing themselves to all that marriage entails. Specifically, they must fully intend three things: 1) fidelity; 2) permanence; 3) openness to children. These three "ends" of marriage are essential. This means that as a couple professes their vows, they must make the interior choice to be completely open to these three ends of marriage.

An obvious example of the lack of total consent would be the couple who are of child bearing age who agrees ahead of time not to have any children. The intentional choice to exclude the possibility of children actually excludes the formation of the marriage bond. In this case, there is an intention against marriage itself by intending to exclude one of the three essential ends of marriage.

**Annulments**: At times, marriages fail and end in civil divorce. In this case, it's important for a couple to have the Church examine their marriage bond in the light of our faith and teaching on the ends of marriage. This process is called an annulment.

Annulments can be very healing and helpful to couples who have experienced divorce. They are healing because the goal of an annulment process is to analyze the marriage bond in the light of the truth. The totality of the consent, the freedom of the consent and the three ends of marriage are, in a sense, put on trial. Did the bond actually take place or not? Was something essential missing from the marriage from the very beginning? These questions must be analyzed in the light of our faith and the teachings of our Church on marriage. In an annulment process, one or both of the persons involved in divorce invites the Church to enter in and make a judgment on the validity of the marriage bond. Though this can be painful to go through, it is almost always healing in the end. It's healing because the persons know that the Church has listened and helped them sort things out.

After thoroughly analyzing the marriage bond, the Church comes back with one of two judgments. They will declare that either the bond does exist, or it doesn't. In the latter case, a judgment of nullity is issued which means that the Church found that something essential was missing from the consent from the very beginning of the marriage. Therefore, the bond of marriage never took place. As a result, the persons are still free to enter into marriage and can do so within the Catholic Church.

Annulments are not a form of Catholic divorce because the Church does not have the authority to separate two validly married people. Rather, an annulment seeks only to clarify what is or is not there.

## A Sacrament or Not

In order to properly understand marriage, it's important to first offer some further clarity on the types of marriage. The primary distinction in marriage is whether it is a sacrament or not. From there, we will also explore marriage between two Catholics, one Catholic and a non-Catholic Christian, and two non-Catholic Christians.

**Marriage on the Natural Order:** As explained earlier in this chapter, marriage was part of the original intention of God and, therefore, is part of the natural order. Jesus elevated marriage to the order of grace, making it a sacrament, for couples who are both baptized. However, when one or both of the persons are not baptized, the marriage is not a sacrament but is still a marriage on the natural order.

What's the difference? In a marriage of the natural order there is still a bond established by the free consent of the couples as outlined earlier in this chapter. The consent must still be free and total and include all three ends of marriage. However, being of a natural order rather than a sacrament simply means that the sacramental grace is not present to that marriage. It doesn't mean God is not present, it just means that the unique grace of the Sacrament is not present. Ideally, God must still be invited into that marriage and the love of God must still assist the couple in their marriage. And if, in the future, both persons become baptized, the natural marriage bond automatically is elevated to the level of a sacrament. Baptism is the gateway to the life of the Sacraments and, therefore, enables marriage to share in this sacramental grace.

**Marriage as a Sacrament:** When both persons are baptized, their marriage is automatically a sacrament. This is the case when marriage takes place between two Catholics, a Catholic and a non-Catholic Christian, or two non-Catholic Christians. In fact, even if two non-Catholic Christians get married by the Justice of the Peace, their marriage is still a sacrament. Only Catholics are bound by the Church to have their marriage vows received in the Church according to the Catholic ritual. All other marriages are recognized as the Institution of Marriage as long as the consent is free and total.

## The Domestic Church

One last aspect to highlight within marriage is the understanding that marriage, as a sacrament, establishes a "Domestic Church." It is God's plan that the family be a place of holiness and unity. The family is the foundational building block of the Church and all of society.

Within the family, children are nurtured, spouses are strengthened, extended relatives have a sense of belonging, and God is made manifest. The family must be seen as a true gift from God and a true source of God's presence and sustaining grace.

The Domestic Church, the family, must be open to and extend to all. For example, those who are single, with no family of their own, must be included in human families. Through friendships and inclusion, all persons must find that they belong not only to God's one divine family, but also to those individual manifestations of God's family within particular domestic churches.

**10**

# AN INTRODUCTION TO PRAYER

Prayer comes from the heart. It goes beyond our minds and takes place in the deepest recesses of our souls. It's something that changes us from within because it's an encounter with the living God living within us. It involves a complete surrender of our entire self to God.

One of the most important parts of prayer is humility. Let's start with that to understand the disposition we must achieve.

### Humility as the Foundation of Prayer

> He then addressed this parable to those who were convinced of their own righteousness and despised everyone else. "Two people went up to the temple area to pray; one was a Pharisee and the other was a tax collector. The Pharisee took up his position and spoke this prayer to himself, 'O God, I thank you that I am not like the rest of humanity—greedy, dishonest, adulterous—or even like this tax collector. I fast twice a week, and I pay tithes on my whole income.' But the tax collector stood off at a distance and would not even raise his eyes to heaven but beat his breast and prayed, 'O God, be merciful to me a sinner.'" (Luke 18:9-13)

Notice in this parable that the Pharisee spoke his prayer to <u>himself</u>, not to God. This shows that pride destroys our life of prayer. On the other hand, notice the beautiful prayer of the tax collector. He was filled with the utmost humility and spoke from the depths of his heart begging God for mercy. He also acknowledged himself to be a sinner. It is as a result of this humility that the tax collector's prayer was truly heard.

Humility is simply knowing and expressing the truth about ourselves and about God. And the truth is that we are sinners in need of God's mercy. But when we know this, and humbly beg for mercy, God lavishes it upon us.

For example, imagine that someone hurt you deeply through their own fault. Now imagine if they came and, somewhat arrogantly said, "Well, I'm sorry you were offended by this, I hope you'll get over it." That's not much of a healing apology. But if they were to come to you in tears saying, "I am truly sorry; I have sinned against you and hurt you through my own fault. Please forgive me. I am truly sorry." In this case, the opportunity for you to forgive and show mercy is much greater.

God hears our prayers when we humble ourselves before Him and beg for mercy. In fact, He is anxious to forgive and heal us. He wants to be reconciled with us. This starting point and foundation of prayer will then lead to so much more. But without this humility as a foundation, it will be hard to move deeper.

## Prayer in the Old Testament

Prayer in the Old Testament is marked by an attempt to enter into a relationship of trust with God. Abraham, for example, is called to have faith and trust in God. He is the "Father of Faith" because he had to believe that God would be faithful to him and his descendents.

Moses also had to respond to God in faith, trusting that God would use him to set His people free and establish a new covenant with them. Moses, especially, is a model of intercessory prayer in that he prayed for God's people when they turned away.

Once the covenant of Moses was established (the Ten Commandments), the kings, especially David, prayed to God in the presence of those Commandments held by the Ark of the Covenant. Eventually the Temple was built and became a place of prayer and worship of God.

The prophets sought the face of God in prayer and relayed God's message of repentance to His people.

Lastly, we see in the Psalms the "masterwork of prayer in the Old Testament." These Psalms reveal both a deeply personal prayer as well as a communal nature of prayer. The people prayed them together, but the prayers themselves were often filled with cries of personal love, adoration, worship, repentance and trust. Over and over again, the Psalms expressed a trust in God's gift of salvation coming in the person of the Messiah.

## Prayer in the New Testament

The witness of prayer in the New Testament is seen in three ways. It's seen in Jesus Himself, in our Blessed Mother and in the early Church.

**Mother Mary:** First, we have the example of our Blessed Mother. Her prayer is the perfect prayer and expresses her whole Immaculate nature. We see this in her fiat, her Magnificat, her intercession with Jesus at the Wedding of Cana and in her adoration of Jesus on the Cross.

Our Blessed Mother's fiat was the foundational prayer of her whole life and should be seen as the perfect model of prayer for our lives. Mary said, "Behold, I am the handmaid of the Lord. May it be done to me according to your word" (Luke 1:38).

Why is this the perfect prayer? Because it expresses humility, trust and surrender. These are the keys to true prayer. It expresses humility in that she acknowledges she is the "handmaid" or the "servant" of the Lord. She also expresses this humility in the Magnificat when she proclaims, "For he has looked upon his handmaid's lowliness…" (Luke 1:48). There is also an expression of trust in that our Blessed Mother embraces the will of God even though it is beyond what she can comprehend. And along with this trust she surrenders to the divine will and plan. This surrender of hers is a choice to embrace the will of God totally. She chooses it in blind faith and confidence, embracing the will of God as her own.

Our Blessed Mother is also the perfect intercessor. First, as a result of her being THE instrument through which Salvation Himself came into the world, she is the instrument and Mediatrix of Grace. She is the channel through which all grace flows. This gives her the supreme function of being the perfect intercessor. Since she is the channel of grace, she has the unique privilege of dispensing grace according to her heart which is always in union with the will of God. But it's important to understand that God does choose to have her be this instrument and intercessor. Therefore, we should acknowledge her role and trust in her intercession and mediation.

Her intercession is first found in John's Gospel when she interceded with Jesus at the Wedding of Cana. They were out of wine and Mary turned to Jesus to ask His help. Jesus, of course, embraced the request of His mother in this instance which is a sign that he always answers her prayers.

Lastly, our Blessed Mother is a model of faith and trust for us as we contemplate her presence at the Crucifixion. She stood there at the Cross and gazed upon her Son as he gave His life. We should see in this gaze her perfect surrender to this divine plan and her mutual offering of her Son to the Father. Her initial fiat at the Incarnation would have been spoken once again, in the depths of her heart, as she watched Jesus fulfill the Father's plan. This willing embrace of her Son's suffering, and the gift of her own suffering in union with her Son's, is the ultimate model of prayer once again. This is especially the case when we are called to give of our lives sacrificially for the love of others.

**Jesus' Prayer**: Jesus is also the perfect model of prayer. But He is actually more than a model; He is also the one in whom we learn to pray. We pray through Him, with Him and in Him. Jesus is seen praying a filial prayer to the Father numerous times. This is especially evident in John's Gospel. It is also evident by the fact that He spent many long nights in prayer alone in solitude. And it's seen very clearly in the Agony of the Garden.

In the Agony of the Garden we see the perfect manifestation of humility and surrender in Jesus. He is suffering greatly as He contemplates what is to come. But rather than give into fear, He prays to the Father, "My Father, if it is not possible that this cup pass without my drinking it, your will be done!" (Matthew 26:42). He humbled Himself by becoming obedient to death, death on a Cross. And He willingly surrendered to the Father's perfect plan for the salvation of the world. This surrender, expressed with His human heart, is the ideal prayer we must all pray. And we can now pray it if we allow Jesus to live in us praying that prayer through us.

Jesus also teaches His disciples to pray. He does this through his own witness of prayer, through His teaching, through the teaching of the Lord's Prayer, and by the witness of His ultimate prayer – His willing sacrifice on the Cross. The prayer of His sacrifice is the perfect prayer and is instituted as a sacrament by Jesus at the Last Supper. It is the institution of this Sacrifice of the Mass that becomes the perfect prayer the disciples learn from Jesus and continue to offer through Him, with Him and in Him.

**The Church at Prayer:** After Pentecost, the Church begins to pray. This is seen in the communal gatherings of the Eucharist as well as in various holy witnesses to Christ. For example, regarding communal prayer, we read in the Acts of the Apostles that "They devoted themselves to the teaching of the apostles and to the communal life, to the breaking of the bread and to the prayers" (Acts 2:42).

Personal witnesses of prayer are also seen in the early Church. For example, St. Stephen the first martyr, prays a perfect prayer of trust and surrender as he is being stoned. He prays, "Lord, Jesus, receive my spirit" and "Lord, do not hold this sin against them" (Acts 7:59-60).

## Basic Forms of Prayer

**Blessing**: First, our prayers rise to the Father in Christ and by the power of the Holy Spirit. To bless God means that we offer up this worship and praise of Him, adoring Him and letting this blessing rise to the Father. Additionally, we are blessed by God in that His grace descends upon us as we bless Him.

**Adoration**: To adore God is to be in His presence with an interior solitude and love. It means we are aware of God's divine presence not only intellectually, but are also attentive to Him with all the powers of our soul. Our whole being is moved with love toward God and an acknowledgment of His divinity, majesty and glory.

**Petition**: First of all, our petition is for mercy and forgiveness. We always need to pray that prayer. From there, we must continually petition God for every good thing. But we must be careful to understand this correctly! Often, it is easy to simply pray for what WE think is good. True petition seeks only the fulfillment of the Kingdom of God on earth. It seeks the will of God and only the will of God. The ultimate petition to God is, "Thy Kingdom come, Thy will be done."

**Intercession**: We are called to intercede for the needs of all people. Our prayers are efficacious. Why? Because God desires to use us as mediators for others. He uses the saints, especially our Blessed Mother, but also wants to use us as intercessors for the needs of others. This reveals the great communion we share with all Christians in that our bond with them, in Christ, enables us to be instruments of grace for others through our prayers.

**Thanksgiving**: All is a gift and all is grace. This should move us to an attitude of thanksgiving. Thanksgiving is an appropriate response to God in all that He has done for us.

**Praise**: Closely associated with thanksgiving, praise of God is given because God is God and is worthy of all praise. Praise is given not so much because of what God has done for us, rather, it is given simply because God is worthy of praise. The Psalms, especially, highlight the form of praise that should be given to God.

### The Holy Spirit Teaches Us to Pray

As Christians, it's important that we humbly realize we do not know how to pray as we ought, nor are we able to pray as we ought by our own ability. It is the responsibility of the Holy Spirit to teach us to pray and to enable us to pray as we ought. Below are various ways that The Holy Spirit has taught us to pray in the life of the Church.

**The Word of God**: The Word of God is alive and is a way God is present to us. By reflecting upon the Word of God, which was inspired by the Holy Spirit, we are engaging Christ Himself, the full revelation of the Father. Since the Word of God is the work of the Holy Spirit, our meditation upon His Word is a clear and practical way that the Holy Spirit guides us in prayer. So, if you want to be taught to pray, spend time reading and meditating upon the Scriptures. Read them slowly, meditatively and prayerfully. As you do, let God speak to you and reveal His presence to you.

**The Liturgy of the Church**: The Liturgy is an act of Christ and His Church. Therefore, every time we engage the Liturgy, we are engaging Christ Himself. We meet Him, discover Him, are fed by Him and grow in love of Him. The Liturgy is a true encounter with God and we must let Him speak to us through our participation in it.

**Virtues of Faith, Hope, and Charity**: True prayer fills us with the virtues of faith, hope and charity. Faith is a true knowledge of God which can only come in the form of prayer. Without true prayer, we can believe things *about* God, but we cannot believe *in* God. Faith is the gift that enables us to see Him and know Him.

Hope produces within our souls a longing for God and a confidence that He is there. We are given a drive to seek Him more deeply and to enter more fully in our trust of Him. Hope energizes us in our relationship with God and is only possible by the power of the Holy Spirit.

Love of God is the ultimate goal of prayer. Through true prayer we come to not only know God and hope in Him, we are also moved to a deep and sustaining love of Him. Love of God means we are united with Him not only in our minds, but also our wills. Love of God produces a strong communion (union) with Him.

## Three Forms of Prayer

> The Lord leads all persons by paths and in ways pleasing to him, and each believer responds according to his heart's resolve and the personal expressions of his prayer. However, Christian Tradition has retained three major expressions of prayer: vocal, meditative, and contemplative. They have one basic trait in common: composure of heart. This vigilance in keeping the Word and dwelling in the presence of God makes these three expressions intense times in the life of prayer. (*CCC* #2699)

**Vocal**: When something is spoken, this is an action on our part. By speaking prayers, speaking praises, individually and communally, we are actively allowing the Holy Spirit to come to us and turn our words into authentic communication with God. There are numerous prayers written by the great saints that express appropriate petitions and praises. These prayers are often the work of the inspiration of the Holy Spirit. So a good place to start is to pray the wonderful prayers of the saints, pray the psalms, or join in the Liturgy and pray it aloud. God will take these prayers and turn them into true prayer.

**Meditation**: Meditation is a way for us to take the revealed Word of God deeper. It is not only a speaking of God's Word, it's also a deep interiorizing of it. By meditating we are letting the Voice of God sink in. It's like a gentle and sustained rain on the crops. The slow and steady nature of this form of rain allows the water to sink deep into the soil so as to nourish the roots. So it is with meditation, it's a way of letting the Word of God sink in deeply so as to nourish our soul.

**Contemplation**: Contemplation is actually the ideal form of prayer and should be considered "True Prayer." It's true prayer because contemplation is not something we can do by ourselves. Contemplation often comes about after we have spent time in meditation allowing God's Word to sink in. Suddenly, there is a moment when our prayer moves from something we are doing, to something God is doing. Contemplation means that God engages our soul and takes over our prayer, mind and will. As St. Paul said, "I live, no longer I, but Christ lives in me" (Galatians 2:20). This expresses the fact that God had taken possession of St. Paul's soul. Christ was living in him. This is prayer and this is the way we are called to live each and every day. In fact, contemplation is how we "Pray without ceasing" (1 Thessalonians 5:17). Ideally, we spend time regularly immersed in God's presence by setting aside time where all we do is pray. In these moments, we hope to be drawn into contemplation and to remain in this intimate and personal union with our God. But contemplation must then extend to our daily life. We must be contemplatives in the midst of action. We must go about our day immersed in the presence of God. We must keep our relationship with Him alive. This continual relationship of contemplation will sustain us and renew us; it will enliven us and enable us to walk in God's presence no matter what we do. And it will enable us to pray always without ceasing.

## Struggles with Prayer

Prayer is the source of all our strength and virtue. It transforms our lives and enables us to become who we were made to be. This happens because prayer is our lifeline to God. In it we not only meet God, we also allow Him to enter into union with us. God lives in us and we live in Him. This profound and absolute unity is what we are made for.

However, prayer can also, at times, be filled with various struggles. We can allow many things to get in the way of our relationship with God. It's essential to a strong prayer life that we understand those struggles. By understanding them we are in a position to face them and overcome them. Below are various struggles most people will encounter with prayer at one time or another.

**Distraction**: Believe it or not, distraction can be a great benefit to a deepening prayer life. This may be surprising and confusing but it's true.

Distractions can be of many types. Busyness, wandering thoughts, worrying, etc., can all challenge our life of prayer and deep union with God. But they can also help! When a distraction truly distracts us from God and we let the distraction win out, this is a problem. We lose focus and fail to let God do what He wants to in our soul. However, if we find ourselves bombarded with various distractions, and every time one comes our way we turn our attention back to God, this is a victory. In fact, the more we do this the closer we come to God. The reason for this is that prayer is very much about our will. Distractions reveal to us what our wills are attached to. This is the first step in surrendering those distractions over. Say, for example, we are excessively worried about a problem and every time we pray our mind wanders to that problem. What this shows us is that we are too attached to whatever it is we are worrying about. Therefore, victory in prayer would be to acknowledge this worry, face it and surrender it over with our will. This enables us to keep sorting through those things that keep us from God. In fact, if all one did for an hour of prayer was to continually surrender over those things that pop into your mind and concern you, this would be a fruitful time of prayer.

Once our minds are emptied of these many distractions and concerns, our will is more easily able to then rest in the heart of God which is the goal of prayer. We must seek to be at peace with God and rest in Him.

**Dryness**: For those who desire deeply to pray and begin down that road, dryness is sure to come. And this also is normal and actually good. Often times, at the beginning of our relationship with God, we are filled with good feelings and spiritual sweetness. This is God's way of initially drawing us in by filling us with delight. Some may call it a "spiritual high."

As we go deeper into prayer and grow in our relationship with God, dryness is sure to come. Why? Because this is one of God's ways of purifying our prayer and enabling us to surrender to Him. If we pray and love God only because we feel good, this is a problem and leaves us in a very shallow relationship with Him. Dryness is a way for God to strip away the spiritual delight and the good feelings so as to invite us to pray to Him, surrender to Him and worship Him out of a more purified choice. Dryness enables us to say yes to God on a whole new level. We commit ourselves to Him not because it makes us feel good, but because God is worthy of love and worship of Him is good and right. This strengthens our resolve and our covenant with Him. And it enables God to take greater possession of our wills.

So if you find that your prayer is dry and if God seems silent, know that He is most likely calling you to a new level of prayer. He is calling you to love Him regardless of how you feel. This is a necessary process for the purification of our souls.

**Lack of Faith**: Of course there are struggles with prayer that are not good. A lack of faith in God is one of those struggles. A lack of faith means that our minds do not properly know the Truth. As a result, our wills cannot surrender to that Truth. Confusion and erroneous thinking can get in the way and can keep us from God. The way to overcome this temptation is to simply meditate upon that which is true. For example, it would be beneficial to take the prayers of the saints and read them, meditate upon them, and try to make them your prayer. Or, take the Scriptures and meditate upon them, especially the words of Jesus.

The key to knowing that we are praying with faith is the good fruit it produces. When our faith is true, we will find ourselves at peace. We may find that the truth we need to hear and believe is hard to accept, but faith will convince us of that truth and grace will give us what we need to surrender to it. True faith is <u>certain</u>, meaning that we will know it is the voice of God. How will we know? We will just know. So if you find yourself confused, this is a sign that you are not hearing God clearly and are not letting the truth He is speaking sink in. On the flip side, it is also possible to come to a false sense of peace and "certainty" as a result of our pride. But this so called certainty cannot be sustained and, in the end, will leave us angry, resentful, upset, or the like. So seek out the Truth that lasts and sustains you in peace.

**Filial Trust**: Closely related to faith in prayer is trust. We are called to the trust of a child, filial trust. This form of trust is total. For example, think of a small child who is frightened or gets hurt. This child will immediately turn to a parent for comfort and, in that parent's arms, will be consoled. So it is with God, we must turn to Him with all our joys but also with all our needs. And this takes the trust of a child. We must know, with certainty, that God loves us and cares for us. Trust frees us from fear which is necessary if we are to truly pray. Praying without fear means we have so given ourselves over to God that we are completely confident in His love for us. This complete confidence is of the greatest importance in our life of prayer. Without it, our relationship will be very shallow with God. But with complete confidence, our relationship with God will become completely sustaining and purifying.

**Praying Constantly**: As mentioned earlier, under "contemplative prayer," we are called to pray without ceasing. This does not mean that we are saying prayers all day long. Rather, it means that we are continually in communion with God.

The path to prayer without ceasing starts by establishing a regular prayer life every day. By setting aside time to pray every day we allow ourselves intense moments in God's presence. Those moments in which we do nothing other than gaze upon the glory of God, are able to then be extended into our daily life. The goal is to make sure we do not compartmentalize our prayer. We do not have our time for God and then our time for everything else. No, the goal is to set aside some time each day *exclusively* for God, and then to allow that time of prayer to be brought into every other part of our day. This means we are constantly aware of God's presence and the continual promptings of the Holy Spirit in our hearts. We see God in all things, discern His will in all things, act by His grace in all things, and serve Him 24/7. Sure, this may seem like a difficult thing to do but it's not as hard as it sounds. In fact, once a good life of prayer is established, we will find that God is always with us and that we are constantly seeking Him and constantly serving Him in various ways. This is truly the goal of the Christian life.

# 11

# THE LORD'S PRAYER

## A Summary of the Whole Gospel

The Lord's Prayer is, indeed, a summary of the entire Gospel. It is called "The Lord's Prayer" in that Jesus Himself gave it to us as a way of teaching us to pray. In this prayer, we find seven petitions to God. Within those seven petitions we will find every human longing and every expression of faith found within the Scriptures. Everything we need to know about life and prayer is contained in the wonderful prayer.

Jesus Himself gave us this prayer as the model of all prayer. It is good that we repeat the words of the Lord's Prayer regularly in vocal prayer. This is also done in the various sacraments and liturgical worship. However, *saying* this prayer is not enough. The goal is to *internalize* each and every aspect of this prayer so that it becomes a model of our personal petition to God and an entrustment of our entire life to Him.

## The Foundation of Prayer

The Lord's Prayer begins not with a petition; rather, it begins with us acknowledging our identity as children of the Father. This is a key foundation for the Lord's Prayer to be prayed properly. It also reveals the foundational approach we must take in all prayer and in the entire Christian life. The opening statement preceding the seven petitions is as follows: "Our Father who art in Heaven." Let's take a look at what is contained in this opening statement of the Lord's Prayer.

**Filial Boldness**: At Mass, the priest invites the people to pray the Lord's Prayer by saying, "At the Savior's command and formed by divine teaching *we dare to say*..." This "daring" on our part comes from the foundational understanding that God is our Father. Each Christian is to see the Father as my Father. We must see ourselves as God's children and approach Him with the confidence of a child. A child with a loving parent is not afraid of that parent. Rather, children have the greatest trust that their parents love them no matter what. Even when they sin, children know they are still loved. This must be our fundamental starting point for all prayer. We must start with an understanding that God loves us no matter what. With this understanding of God we will have all the confidence we need to call on Him.

**Abba**: Calling God "Father" or, more specifically, "Abba" means we cry out to God in the most personal and intimate of ways. "Abba" is a term of endearment for the Father. This shows that God is not just the Almighty or the All-Powerful. God is so much more. God is my loving Father and I am the Father's beloved son or daughter.

**"Our" Father**: To call God "our" Father expresses an entirely new relationship as a result of the New Covenant that was established in the blood of Christ Jesus. This new relationship is one in which we are now God's people and He is our God. It's an exchange of persons and, therefore, deeply *personal*. This new relationship is nothing other than a gift from God that we have no right to. We have no right to be able to call God our Father. It's a grace and a gift.

This grace also reveals our profound unity to Jesus as the Son of God. We can only call God "Father" in so far as we are one with Jesus. His humanity unites us to Him and we now share in a deep bond with Him.

Calling God "our" Father also reveals the union we share with one another. All who call God their Father in this intimate way are brothers and sisters in Christ. We, therefore, are not only deeply connected together; we also are enabled to worship God together. In this case, individualism is left behind in exchange for fraternal unity. We are members of this one divine family as a glorious gift of God.

**"Who Art in Heaven"**: Acknowledging that God is in Heaven is not so much to say He is away in some "place." It means He is in a glorious state of being. He is not away from us somewhere else. In fact, our acknowledgment of His Heavenly reign actually reveals that we are called to share in that glorious life of God right now. We are the People of God who live united with Christ in this hidden yet glorious Kingdom already established. Our life of prayer is that constant connection to and participation in this Kingdom.

## The Seven Petitions

The Lord's Prayer reveals to us seven petitions. These petitions cover the entire Christian life. Let's look at each one of them so that we will, indeed, know how to pray.

The first three petitions of the Lord's Prayer focus on God. This reveals the essence of love: love always draws us out of ourselves toward the other. These petitions help us to love and adore God and desire His will for His sake. We pray: "Hallowed be thy name...thy Kingdom come...thy will be done."

**Hallowed be Thy Name**: "Hallowed" means to be holy. As we pray this part of the prayer we are not praying that God's name *will* become holy, for His name already *is* holy. Rather, we pray that this holiness of God will be recognized by us and all people. We pray that there will be a deep reverence of God's name and that we will always treat God with the proper honor, devotion, love and awe we are called to.

It's especially important to point out how often God's name is used in vain. That is a strange phenomenon. Have you ever wondered why, when people get angry, they would curse God's name? It's strange. And, in fact, it's demonic. Anger, in those moments, invites us to act in a contrary way to this prayer and to the proper use of God's name.

God Himself is holy, holy, holy. He is thrice holy! In other words, He is the Holiest! Living with this fundamental disposition of heart is key to a good Christian life and to a good life of prayer.

Perhaps a good practice would be to regularly honor God's name. For example, what a wonderful habit it would be to regularly say, "<u>Sweet and precious</u> Jesus, I love You." Or, "<u>Glorious and merciful</u> God, I adore You." Adding adjectives like these before we mention God is a good habit to get into as a way of fulfilling this first petition of the Lord's Prayer.

Another good practice would be to always refer to the "Blood of Christ" we consume at Mass as the "<u>Precious</u> Blood." Or the Host as the "<u>Sacred</u> Host." There are many who fall into the trap of just referring to it as the "wine" or the "bread." This is most likely not malicious or even sinful, but it's much better to enter into the practice and habit of honoring and revering anything that is associated with God, especially the Most Holy Eucharist!

**Thy Kingdom Come**: This petition of the Lord's Prayer is a way of acknowledging two things. First, we acknowledge the fact that Jesus will, one day, return in all His glory and establish His permanent and visible Kingdom. This will be the time of the Final Judgment when the current Heaven and Earth will pass away and the new order will be established. So, praying this petition is a faith-filled acknowledgment of this fact. It's our way of saying we not only believe this will happen, we also look forward to it and pray for it.

Secondly, we must realize that the Kingdom of God is already here among us. For now, it's an invisible Kingdom. It's a spiritual reality that must become an all-consuming and present reality in our world.

To pray that God's "Kingdom come" means we desire that He first take greater possession of our souls. The Kingdom of God must be within us. He must reign on the throne of our hearts and we must allow Him. Therefore, this must be our constant prayer.

We also pray that the Kingdom of God become present in our world. God wants to transform the social, political and cultural order right now. So we must pray and work for that. Our prayer for the Kingdom to come is also a way for us to commit ourselves to God to allow Him to use us for this very purpose. It's a prayer of faith and courage. Faith because we believe He can use us, and courage because the evil one and world will not like it. As the Kingdom of God is established in this world through us, we will meet with opposition. But that's ok and should be expected. And this petition is, in part, to help us with this mission.

**Thy will be done on Earth as it is in Heaven**: Praying for the Kingdom of God to come means, also, that we seek to live the will of the Father. This is done as we enter into union with Christ Jesus. He fulfilled the will of His Father with perfection. His human life is the perfect model of the will of God and it is also the means by which we live the will of God.

This petition is a way of committing ourselves to live in union with Christ Jesus. We take our will and entrust it to Christ so that His will lives in us.

By doing this we begin to be filled with all virtue. We will also be filled with the Gifts of the Holy Spirit which are necessary for living the will of the Father. For example, the Gift of Knowledge is a gift by which we come to know what God wants of us in particular situations in life. So praying this petition is a way of asking God to fill us with knowledge of His will. But we also need the courage and strength necessary to then live out that will. So this petition also prays for those Gifts of the Holy Spirit that enable us to live out what God reveals as His divine plan for our lives.

It is, of course, also an intercession for all people. In this petition we pray that all will come to live in unity and harmony with God's perfect plan.

The next four petitions of the Lord's Prayer still focus upon God, but more directly acknowledge our need of Him and the need for us to offer ourselves to Him as an offering. In these petitions we pray: "Give us...forgive us...lead us...deliver us."

**Give us this day our daily bread**: This petition, like the opening of the Lord's Prayer, expresses our child-like need to trust in God to care for us. It also points to the covenant in that we seek to receive all *from* God as we seek to give all *to* God.

To pray for our "daily" bread is a way of acknowledging that God transcends time and place. He is all present and needed in all time.

And to say, "this day" is a way of inviting God into this present moment, the only moment we have.

"Bread" is certainly a reference to the Holy Eucharist but it is also an acknowledgement that, through the Eucharist and all grace, God is the source of our sustenance. Without Him we starve, literally. Our souls wither and, in fact, without God we could no longer even exist.

We also trust that God will provide for our material needs. No, God may not have as a part of His plan that we become rich in worldly possessions, but we can be assured that He will care for us and provide, materially, and in every other way, for what we do need in life. So this is a prayer of trust in the providence of God.

**Forgive us our trespasses, as we forgive those who trespass against us**: This may be one of the most difficult of the petitions to pray. Forgiveness is two sided. First, God is a God of perfect mercy. There is no sin too big for God to forgive and forget. We must know this. Guilt, shame, embarrassment, and fear must fade away in the presence of God's abundant mercy. We pray for this grace in this petition.

However, the mercy of God works both ways! The only way to receive God's mercy and forgiveness is to give it. And, the extent that we offer mercy and forgiveness is the extent that we open our hearts to receive it. Imagine it this way. Imagine that you are out snorkeling. You are in the tropics exploring the beauty of the sea. In order to do this you need a snorkeling tube to breathe through. When you breathe, you do not use one large one to breathe in and then switch to a small one to breathe out. No, you use the same tube for both. So it is with mercy and forgiveness. We determine how "big" our breathing tube is and we use only one. If we use a straw for forgiving others, we must use that same straw to receive forgiveness. It's our choice. But if we use a full-sized tube as a channel of grace, both to give and receive, we will be very satisfied.

This analogy also shows us that we need mercy and forgiveness. No one can go snorkeling and say, "I'll just hold my breath the whole time. I do not need to breathe" This is like saying, "I will just live my life myself, I do not need regular mercy and forgiveness." This is a dangerous and deadly attitude.

Sometimes we encounter people who do not seem worthy of our forgiveness. They may be arrogant, demanding, hurtful and the like. It matters not. We must offer mercy and forgiveness to them just as we offer it to the sweetest and kindest person we know. It must be total, constant and unconditioned. Remember the words of Jesus on the Cross, "Father, forgive them, they know not what they do" (Luke 23:34).

**And lead us not into temptation**: This line of the Lord's Prayer can be confusing. Why would God "lead us" into temptation? Well, He wouldn't. This is confusing simply because it's hard to translate this Greek line. The *Catechism* explains it this way:

> It is difficult to translate the Greek verb used by a single English word: the Greek means both "do not allow us to enter into temptation" and "do not let us yield to temptation" (Mt 26:41). (#2846)

Temptation is real. We all encounter it. But is it true that some temptations are so severe that we cannot help ourselves? Yes, it's true, sometimes temptations are too much for our own human strength. But fear not, temptations are never too much for the grace of God. Therefore, this petition is a way of saying, "Lord, I am weak and by myself I will fail. Therefore, I entrust myself to You so that I will never be led astray by the many temptations I will certainly face."

When we fall into temptations we can be certain it's because we failed to embrace this particular petition of the Lord's Prayer. We failed to properly seek out and rely upon all that God wants to give us. He is the master of virtue and the conqueror of vice. If we completely turn to Him in the midst of temptation we can be certain that He will come to our side.

**But deliver us from evil**: As we pray that we are delivered from evil, we are actually praying that we are delivered from the devil. Evil, in and of itself, does not exist. Evil is what we call a "negative reality." In other words, evil is the lack of something. It's the lack of God.

By analogy, contrast the difference between light and dark or hot and cold. Are these opposing forces? No. Darkness, in fact, does not exist nor does cold exist strictly speaking. Darkness is simply the absence of light and cold is simply the absence of heat. So it is with good and evil. These are not two opposing forces like we see in Star Wars. Rather, evil is the loss of God and all that is good.

This petition is a way of praying for protection from "the evil one," satan. He is the one who wishes to steal God away from our lives. Satan is real, he is powerful, and he hates us with all his might. As a powerful angel he retains his natural powers of influence over us. But the grace of God has overcome him and when we pray for that grace we can be certain that satan will lose. We must pray to be kept safe from the evil one, from the one who has completely lost God.

And that is prayer! The Lord's Prayer traditionally ends by glorifying God. This glorification of God is what we must do at all times and is a fitting way to end this book:

> *For the kingdom, the power and the glory are yours, now and forever!*

> *AMEN*

# SMALL GROUP STUDY

One of the best ways to learn our glorious Catholic faith is through faith-based small group discussion and study. Talking about our faith brings clarity. Hearing what others have to say brings insight.

Each of the three books of the *My Catholic Life! Series* can be used as an 8 week program of Catholic study for you to engage in. This small group study program is great for these and other settings:

- **Family** – Why not gather family members together for an eight week study of our faith?!
- **Friends** – Initiate a study among your friends and invite some new friends!
- **Neighborhood** – This is a great way to evangelize right in your neighborhood. Send a letter out inviting neighbors. You just may be surprised at how many are interested!
- **Parish** – Talk to your parish priest to gain permission to begin one or more study groups at your local church.
- **R.C.I.A.** – This is a great tool to use for those becoming Catholic. All three series, together, will cover the entire *Catechism*!

**Who can start a program?** – This program is designed to be easy for any Catholic to organize and lead. You do not have to be an expert in the Catholic faith to take the initiative. If you feel called to take this initiative then "Be not afraid" and jump in!

**What do you need?** – The materials include one of the three catechetical books from the *My Catholic Life! Series* as well as the study companion which is available for free online at www.myCatholic.Life/small-group-study. So visit that link, pray, and ask our Lord how He wants you to help spread the faith!

## www.myCatholic.Life

Also, download the "Catholic Daily Reflections" app for smart phones and tablets. Available through website or all app stores.

Made in the USA
Lexington, KY
26 September 2019